Clarence Robert Tower

Painting and Drawing Memories and Memorabilia

(With Photoshop Extras)

Published in the United States of America

ISBN-13: 978-1545083413
ISBN-10: 154508341X

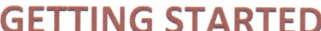
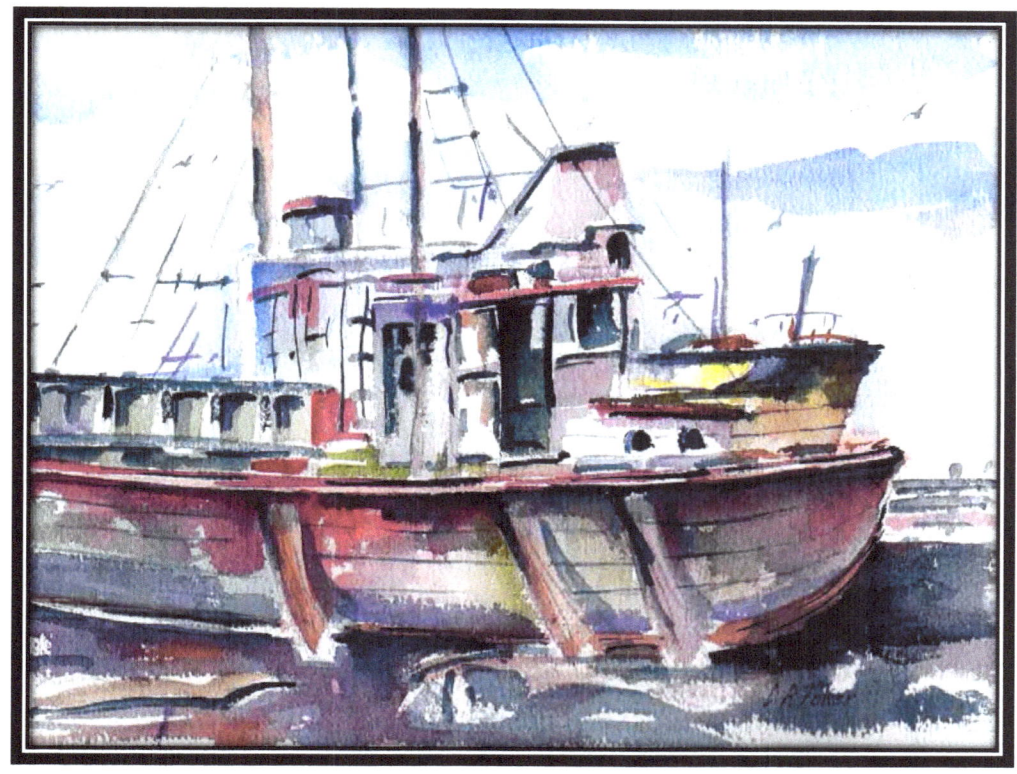

"Moss Landing – Dry Docked"

The paintings shown on this and the following page were completed during my early years of exploring this magical adventure known as painting and drawing. At that particular time, I was constantly reminded by watercolor purists that a loose/wet style was the only style acceptable for a watercolor painting. It didn't take long, however, for me to realize that such was not about to satisfy my ultimate need, which was to enjoy the fine points of detail. (See cover painting for example) This approach would carry on to pen-and-ink drawings, oil paintings and even glass sculpture. With the knowledge of knowing that I spent my professional life preparing recorded documents entirely by hand behind us, this was a pre-set decision.

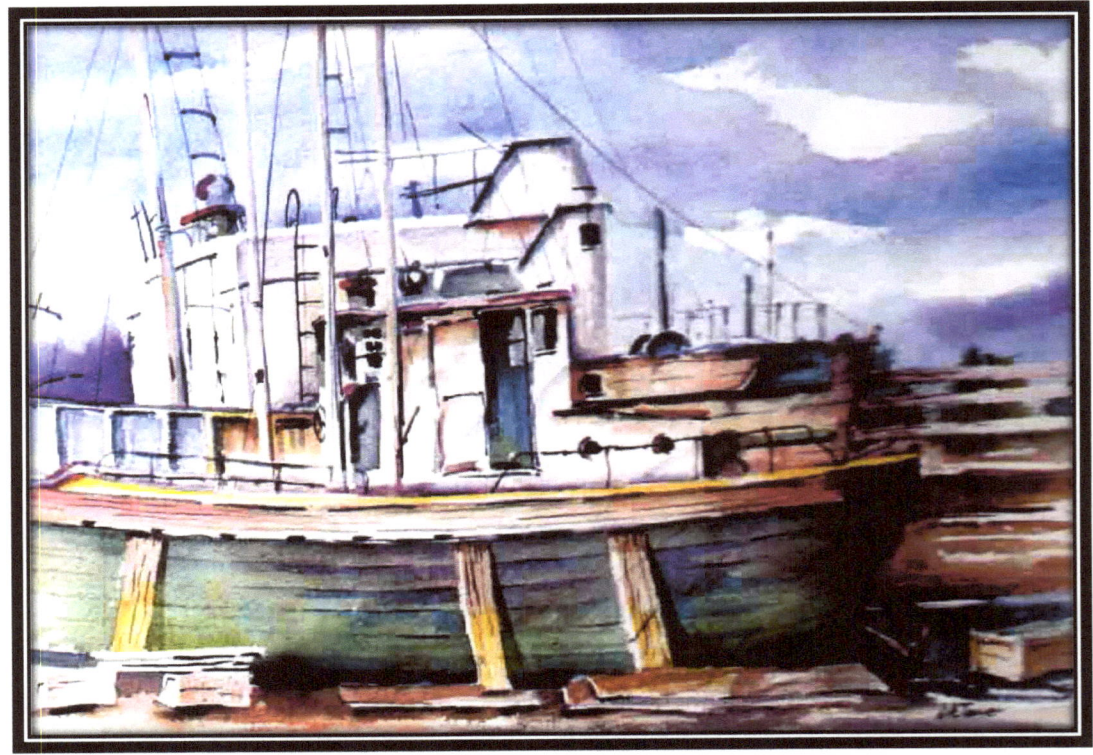

"*Moss Landing – Dry Docked – 2*"

"Dry Docked 1" (shown on the previous page), was an early attempt at a traditional watercolor. I felt at the time that I could produce better results, so I started over and went on to complete "Dry Docked 2." For the record, I was satisfied with both, but clearly felt #2 was an improvement. Regardless, the amount of experience I gained by painting the same painting twice was monumental.

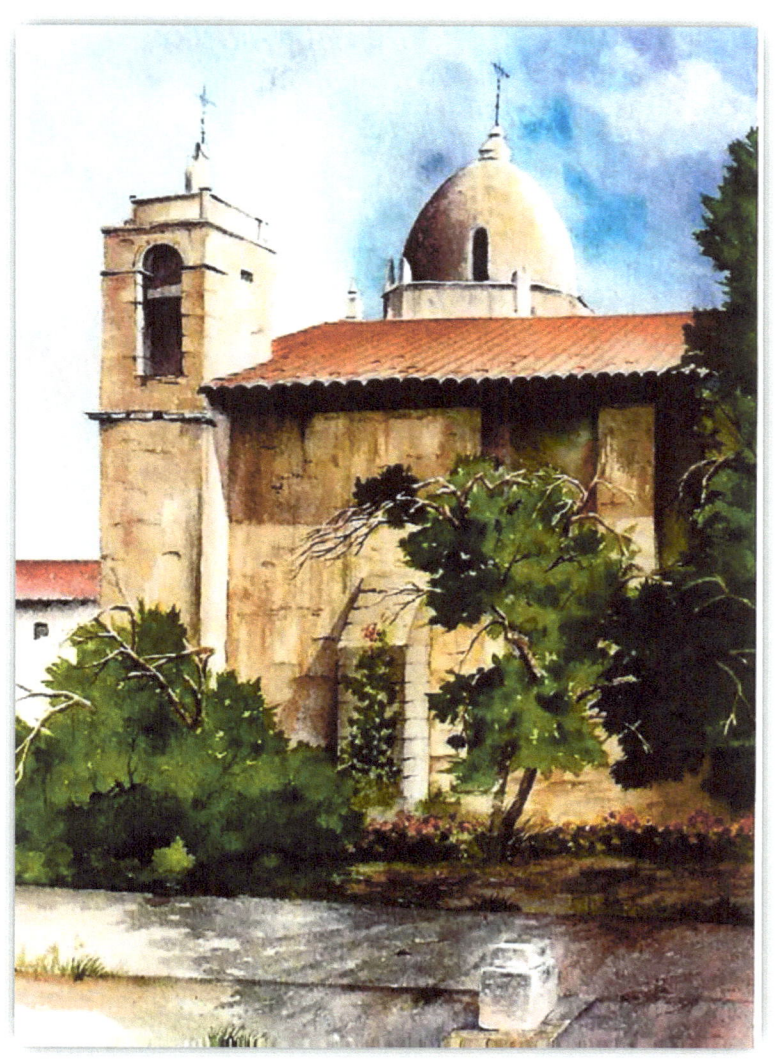

The watercolor painting shown to the left and the one on the following page are lesser seen views of California's Carmel Mission. The one shown here was predominately painted in a wet style, which means the entire painting was completed while the paper was maintained in a damp state. This allows for natural blending between applied wet pigments. This can best be seen by observing the sky and shrubbery, which have a loose, flowing look. Looking further, one can see the soft blend from dark areas to light areas throughout the entire painting.

To the new watercolorist:

The exposed branches seen throughout the shrubbery area are the result of masking off the targeted areas with rubber-based masking fluid which is ultimately removed by a gummy eraser. The removal is done when the painting is dry. This procedure maintains the white background.

See following page for continuation.

The painting to the right differs little in appearance from the one on the previous page, but it does differ in the way it was completed. As was the case with the previous paintings, the major portion was painted on a damp-paper surface. Again, this results in a natural blending of brush applications. In this painting, however, close inspection of the shrubbery shows exact detailing as would be the case with an oil painting, except watercolor pigments were used.

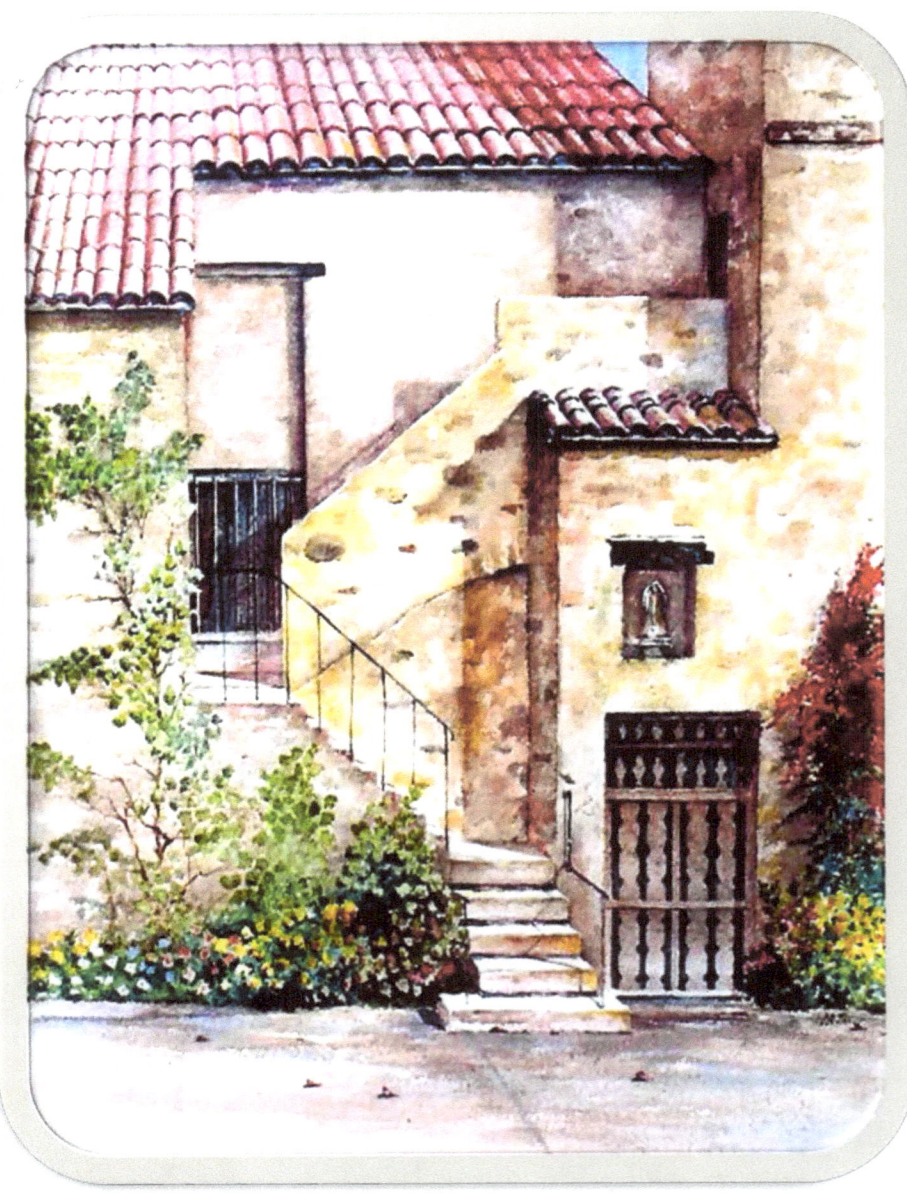

The value of this procedure rests in the reality that an individual can work in a controlled state, as opposed to working wet-on-wet, where said individual has much less control.

ESTABLISHING A STYLE

The painting shown to the right, along with the painting shown on the following page, depict my love for Americana. Adding to that is my natural tendency to love detail. With all this being the case, I found much satisfaction in producing well detailed paintings.

As I touched upon previously, my approach to watercolor painting is much like painting with oil, except for the obvious substitution of the pigment. Watercolor, however, allows the painter to lift the pigment and soften edges when needed to correct problems. This was immensely important to me in my search for a unique style.

I did complete a number of oil paintings, which the reader will see later in the book. However, all involved tedious and disciplined efforts, which did not fit my need for relaxation. With all this said, I will forever cherish the softness of the detail I was able to accomplish with my watercolors.

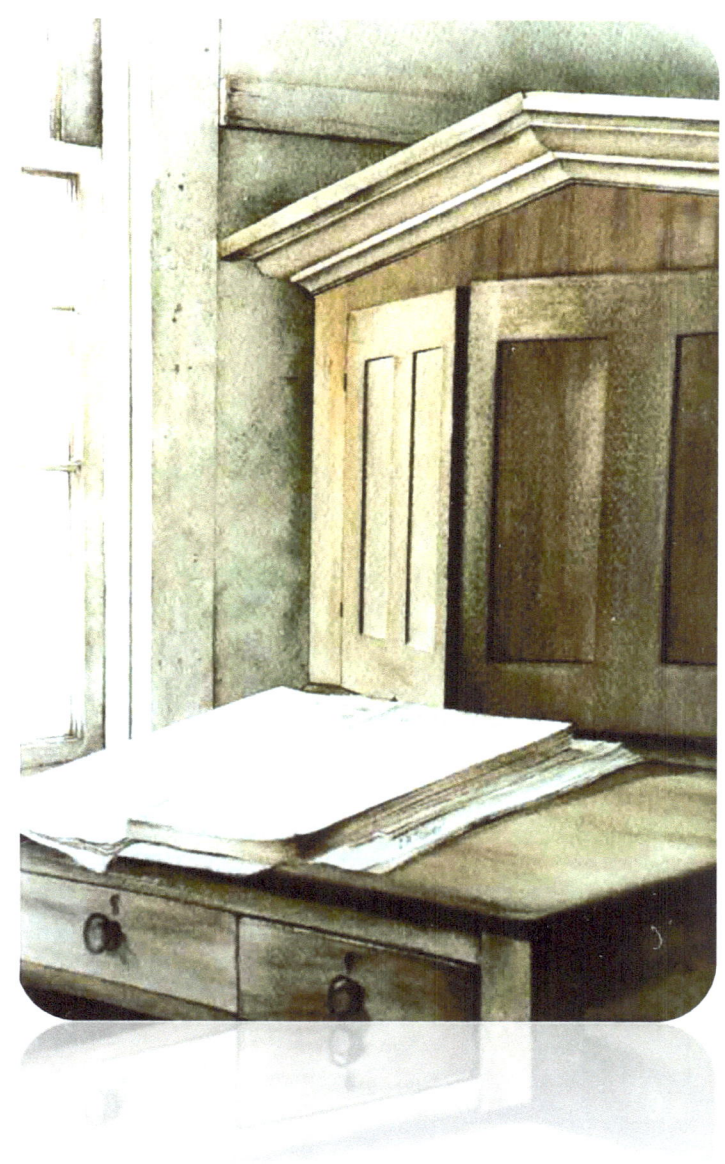

Right: Desk at Woodside Store"
(Woodside, California)

ESTABLISHING A STYLE

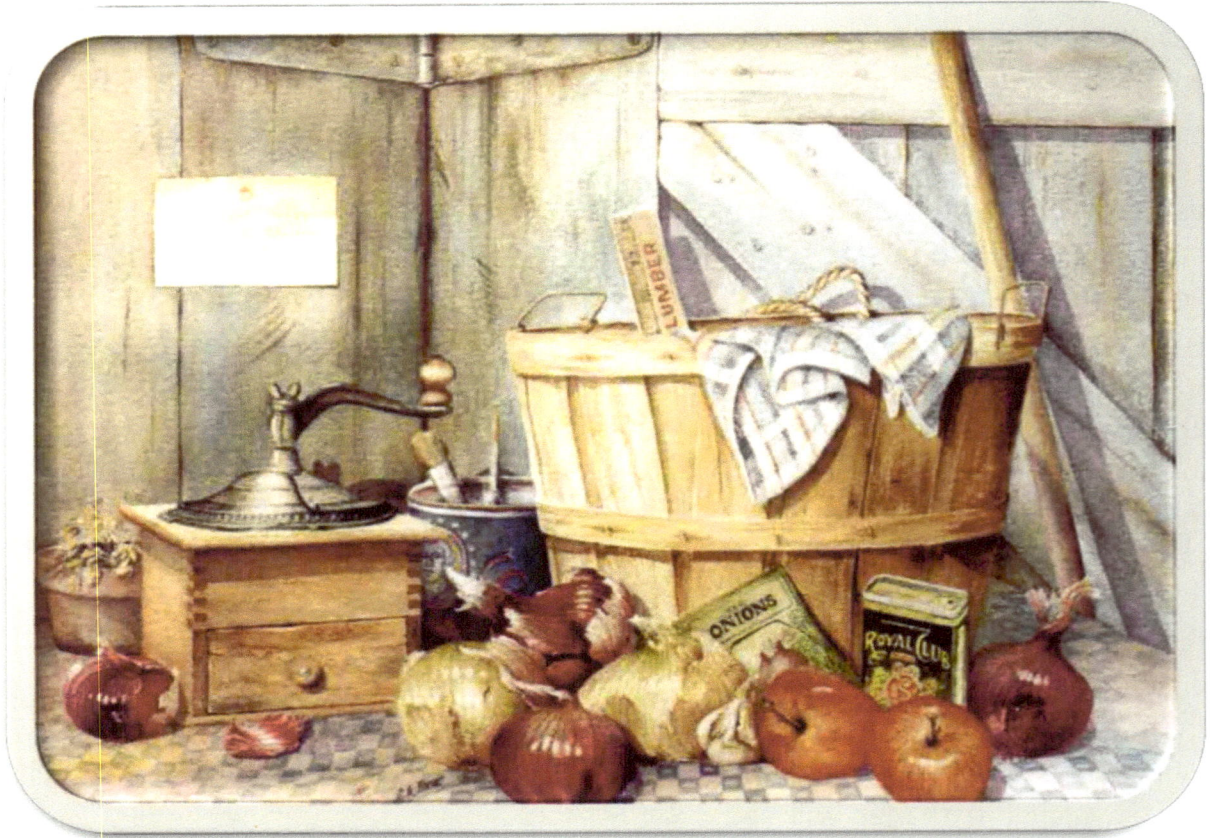

"Apples and Onions"
(From the Americana Series)

SAVING SOURCE MATERIAL

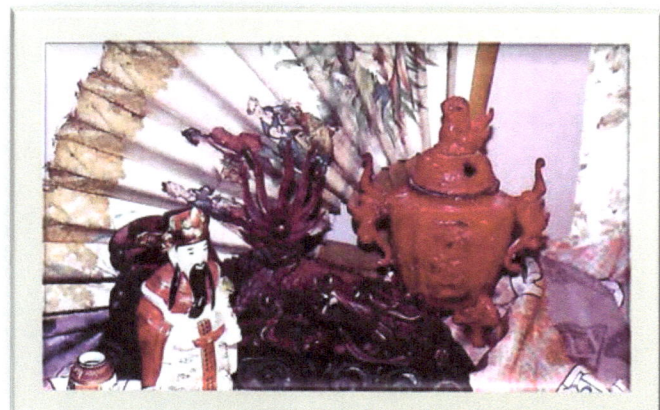

I am often asked if I use photographs to aid me in setting up a composition. The answer is always "Absolutely, yes, without question." The photo in the upper left is one of several I utilized for the "Fan and Pearl" painting shown on the following page.

Notice that the dragon shown below is the very same carved dragon seen in the painting.

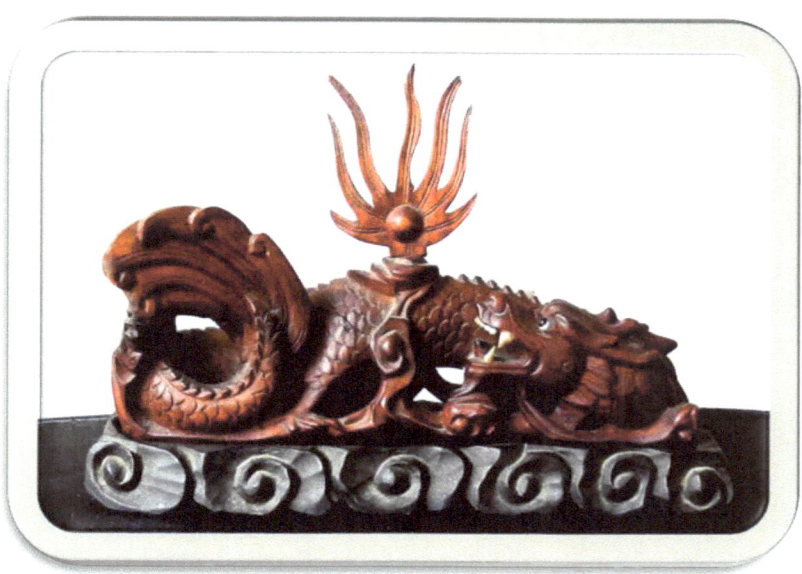

Saving your source material adds immensely to the proof of originality of the work.

One more thing to remember always, "A piece of artwork needs to be accomplished by the artist exclusively to be an original piece, but all that matters, in reality, is the final product hanging on the wall.

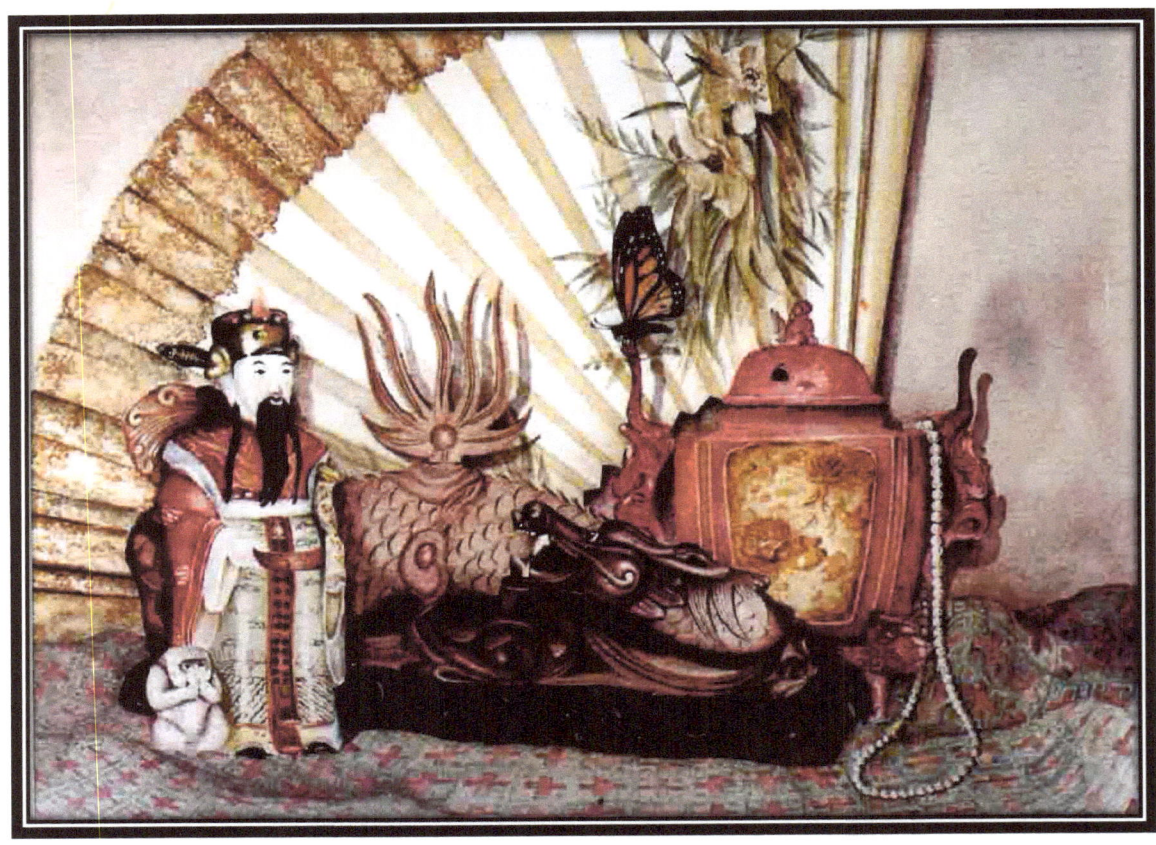

"FAN WITH STRING OF PEARLS"
Watercolor – 22" x 30"

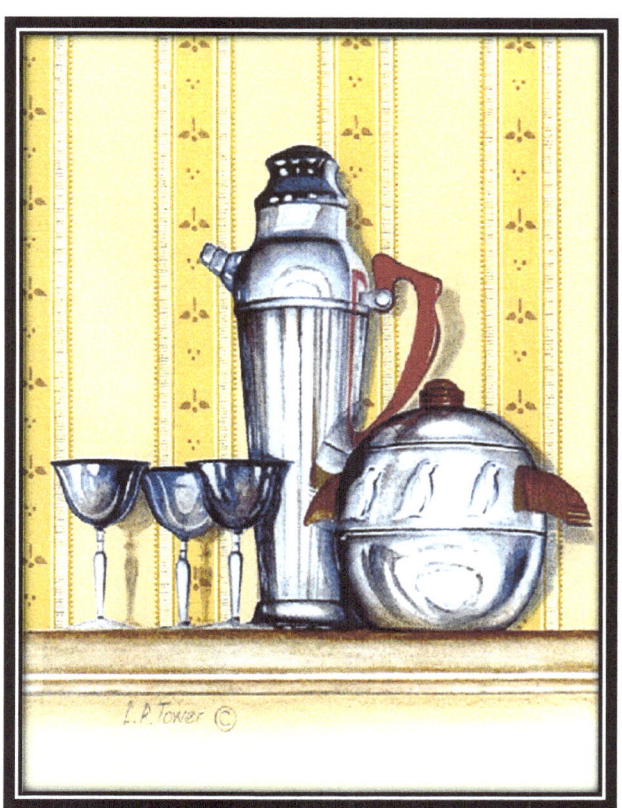

Catching the glistening sheen of chrome is certainly not easy, but the results are definitely worth the effort. These two paintings and the painting on the following page were completed months apart, but I was totally amazed at the similarity of the final results. The background for the painting on the left is not original. It has been photoshopped in.

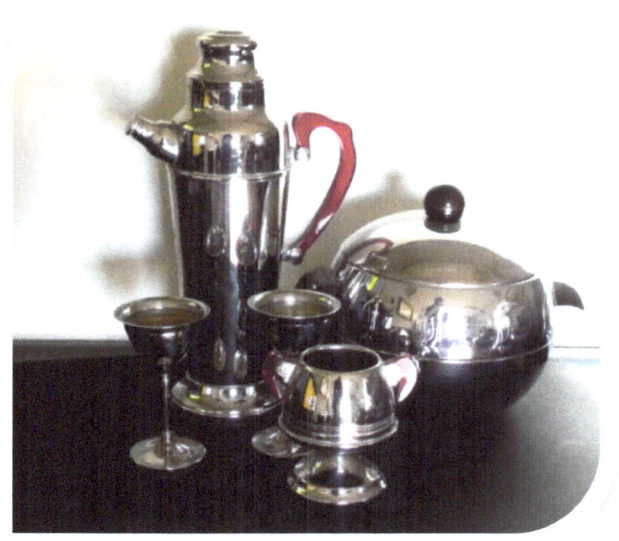

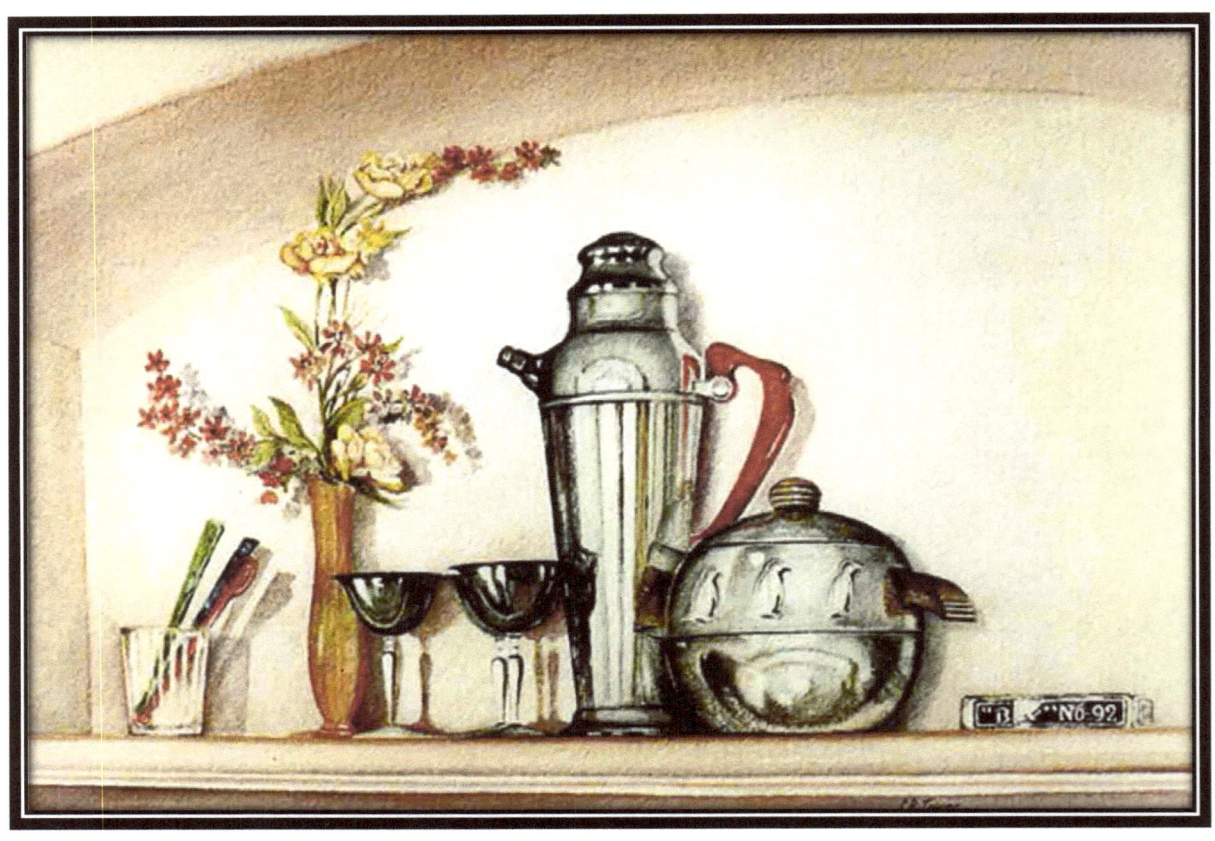

"The Chrome Service"

SAVING SOURCE MATERIAL

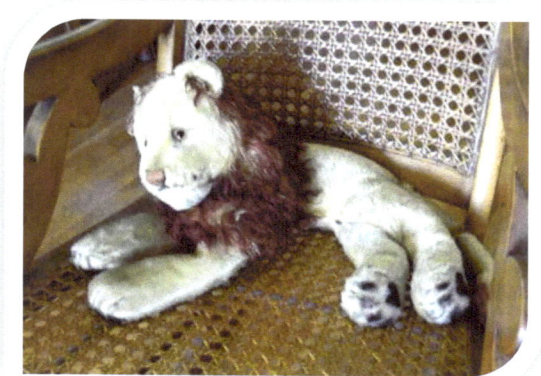

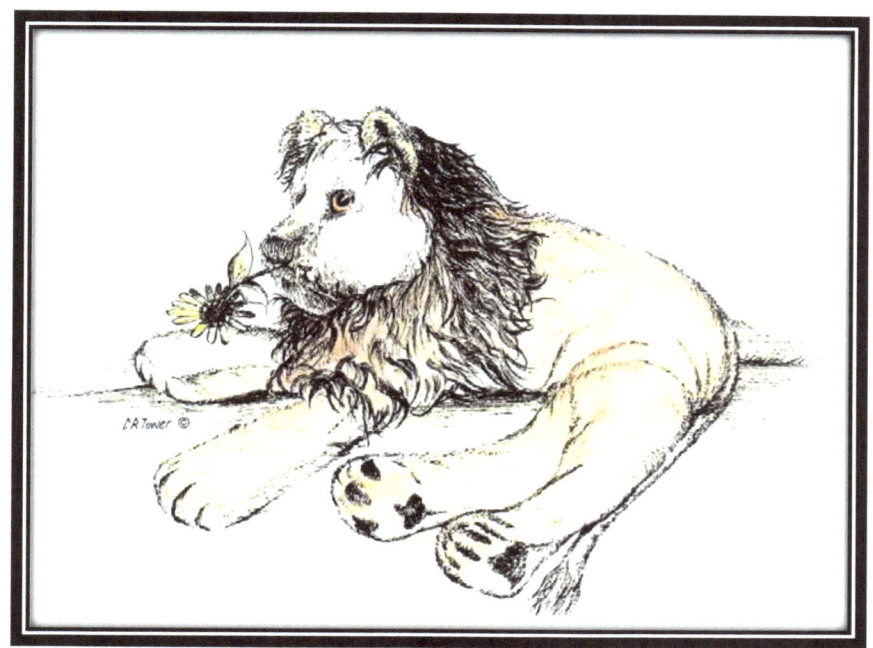

The original "Dandy Lion"

This great stuffed lion has been a member of my family for more than 30 years. He was old and tattered when we found him, but much too lovable to escape being imortalized. (Drawing from my children's book)

SAVING SOURCE MATERIAL

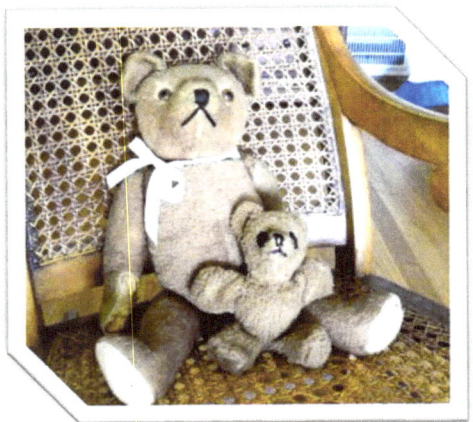

The Original Bears

The smaller of the two has been a close buddy for more than 50 years. Much joy was found in documenting their images.

The larger of the two bears shown above left can proudly claim to have been a member of my family for more than 80 years.

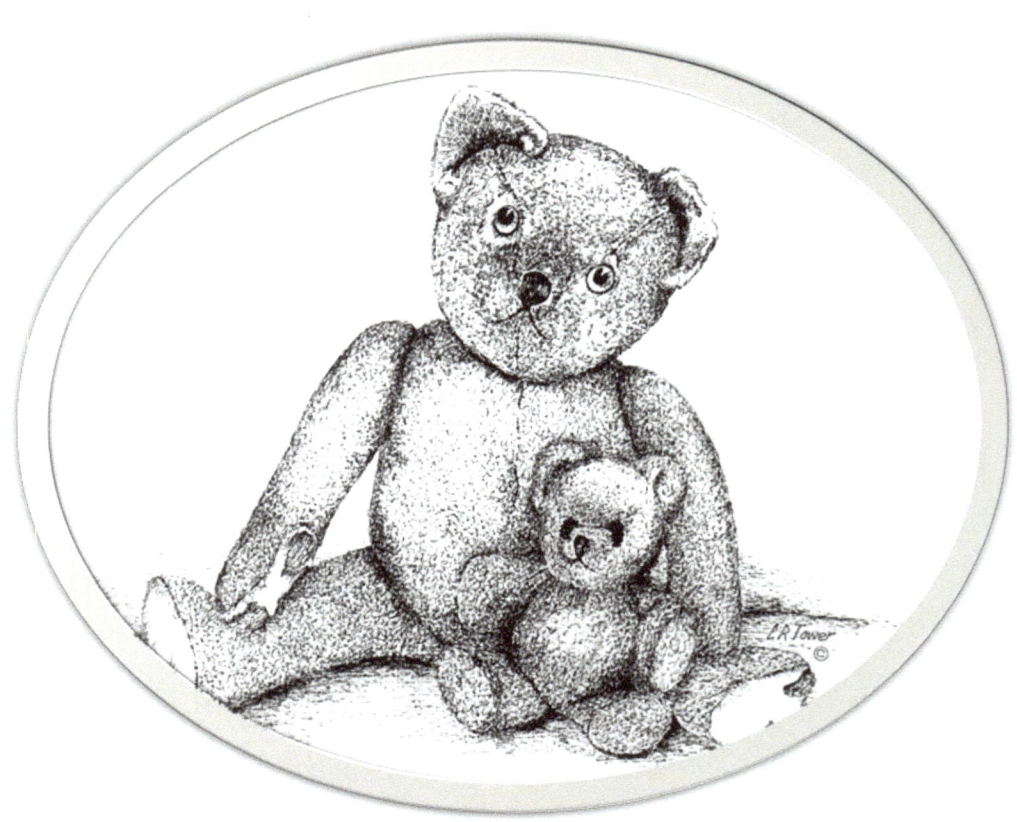

FROM A DISNEY ARTIST

CUT-OFFS – AN IMPORTANT TOOL

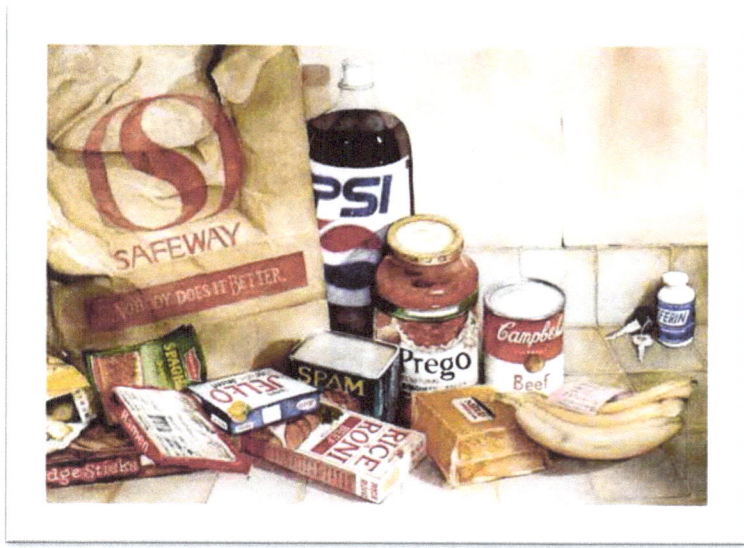

Today's Groceries – Watercolor – 22" x 30"

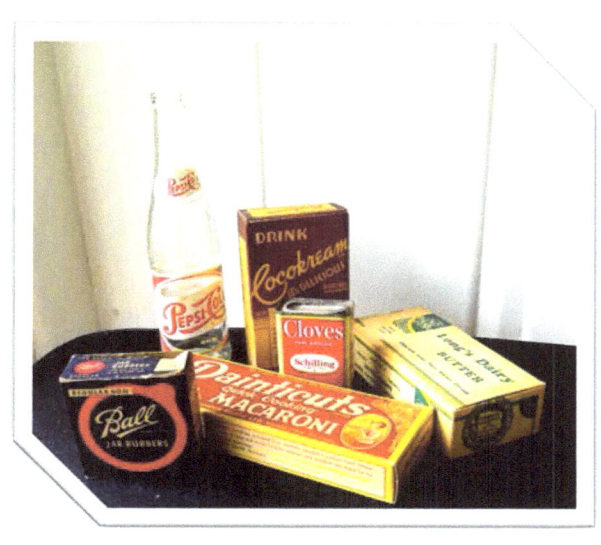

The process of arranging items within a composition so that a selected item masks off a portion of the item located directly behind it, is referred to as a "Cut-Off." Such is used to create the illusion of depth, even when one knows the drawing surface is actually flat. The painting above and the photo at the left are great examples. The very items shown in the photo were previously used for the painting shown on the following page. This lesson in reality was passed on to me by a retired Disney artist.

FROM A DISNEY ARTIST

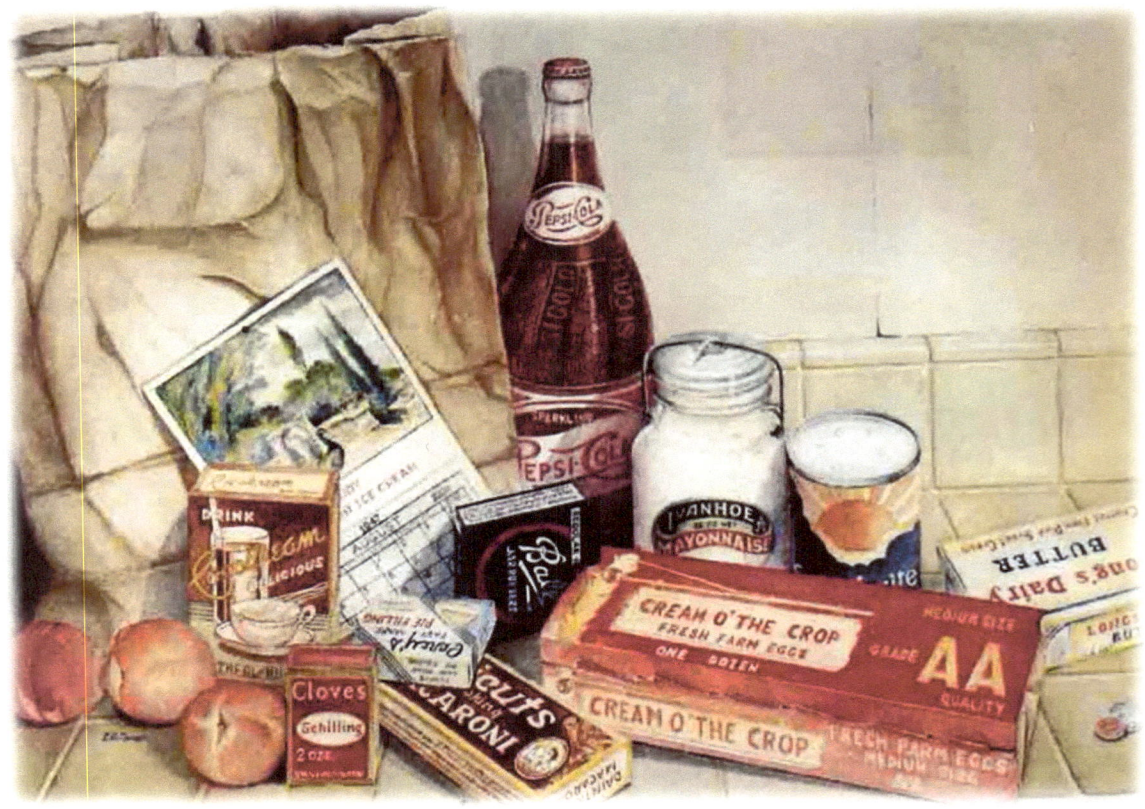

Yesterday's Groceries - Watercolor 22" x 30"

A CHANGE OF PACE

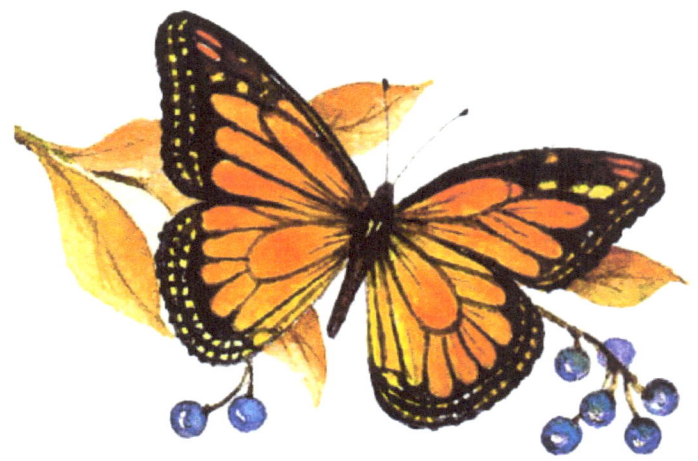

FOLLOWING IS A GALLERY OF HISTORY AND TRAVEL, FAR-AND-NEAR ®

How many people can say they live 200 feet from a California State Historical Landmark?
I can!
It's the C. C. Morse mansion – the house that seeds built.

Being that I live in its shadow,
I found myself challenged to tackle
both this pen and ink drawing and oil painting.
(See drawing and painting on following pages)

As I look back, I now realize this was the beginning
of many more such challenges,
a number of which, readers will see in following pages.

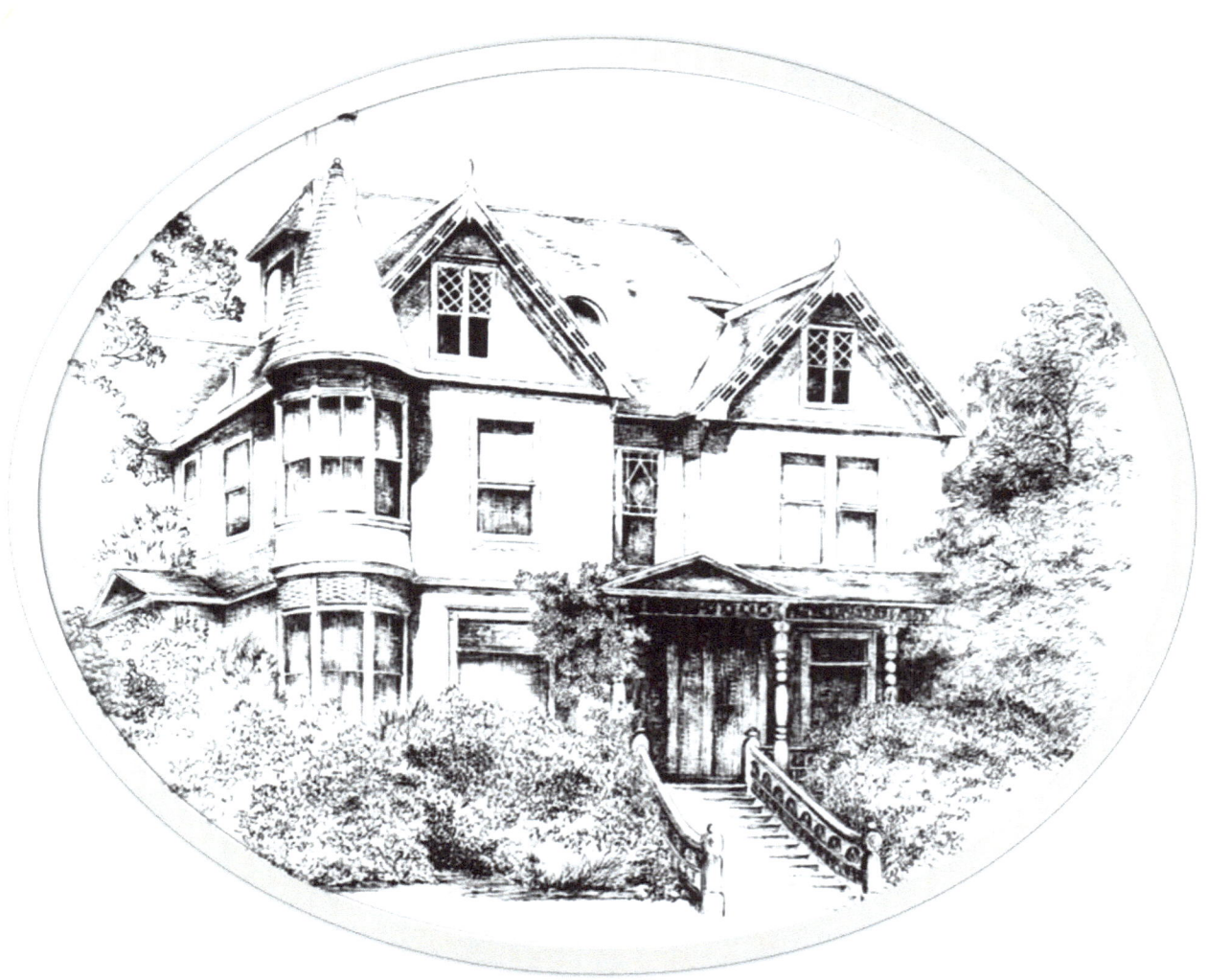

C. C. Morse Mansion
Santa Clara, California
Pen & Ink

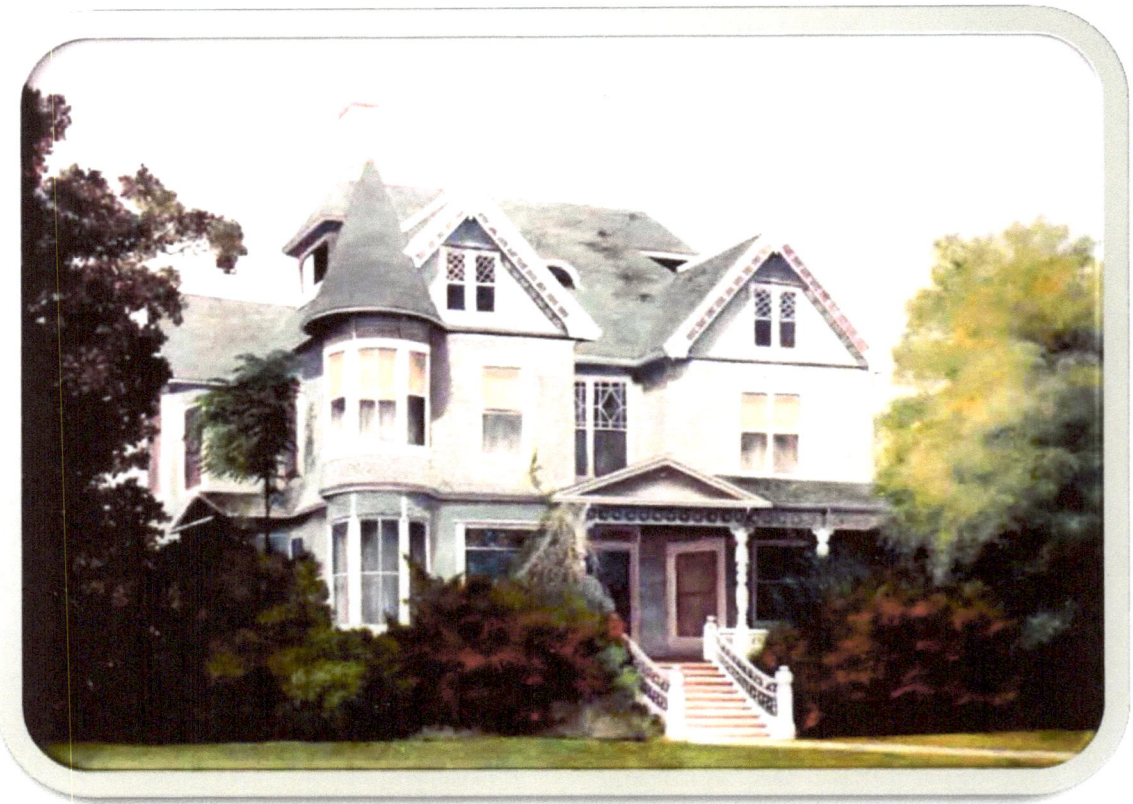

C.C. Morse Mansion
Santa Clara, California
Oil Painting

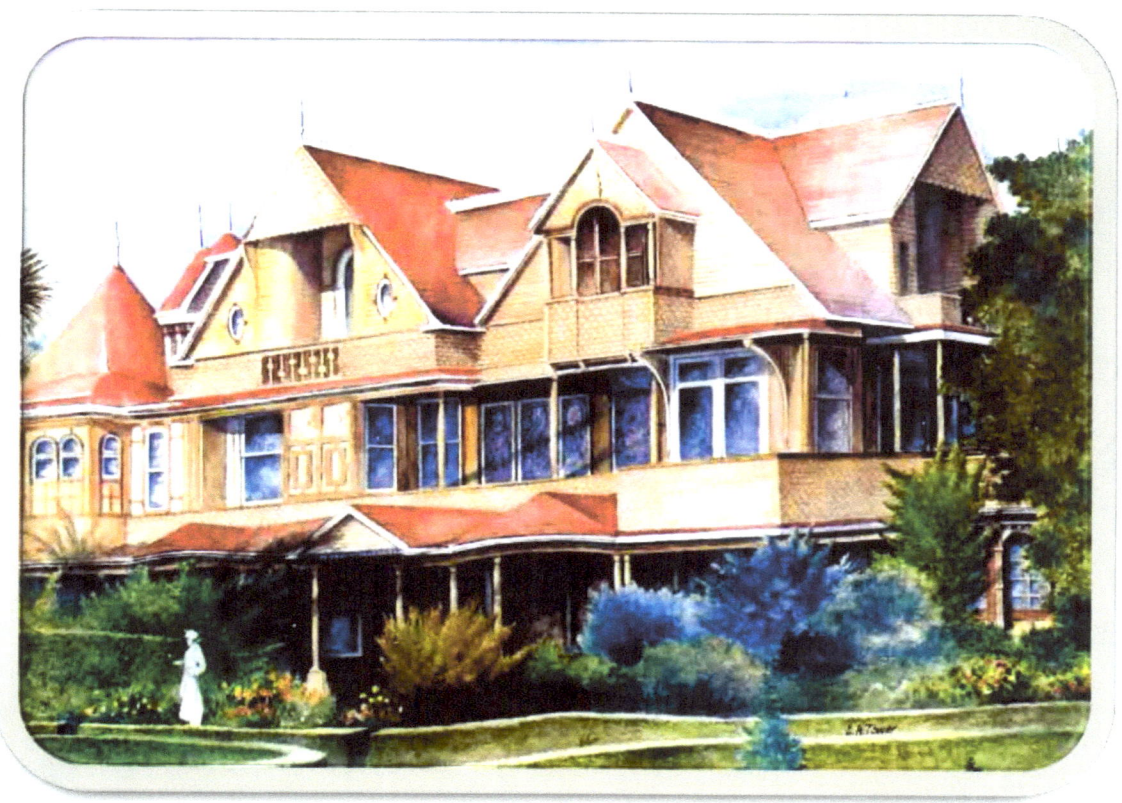

Winchester Mystery House
San Jose, California
Watercolor

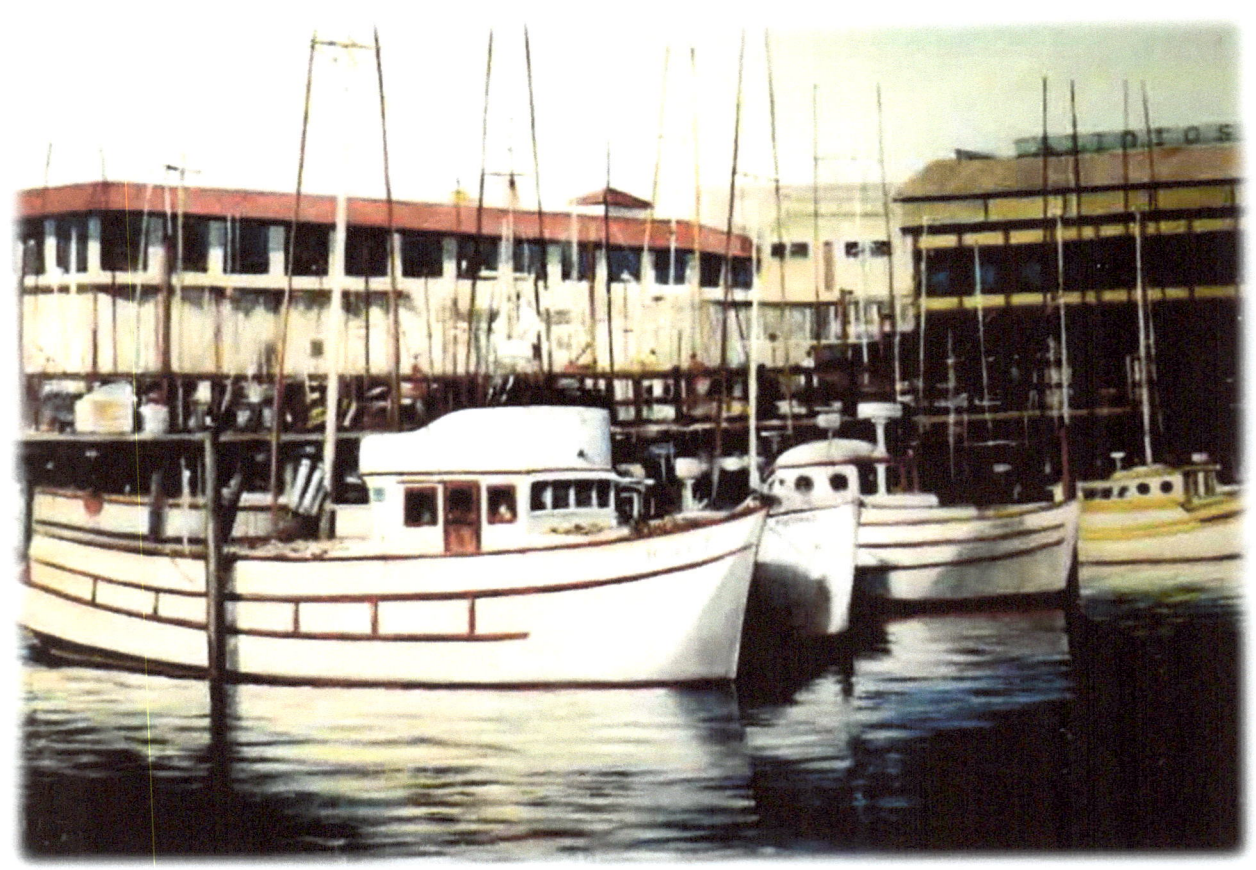

Fisherman's Wharf
San Francisco, California
Oil Painting

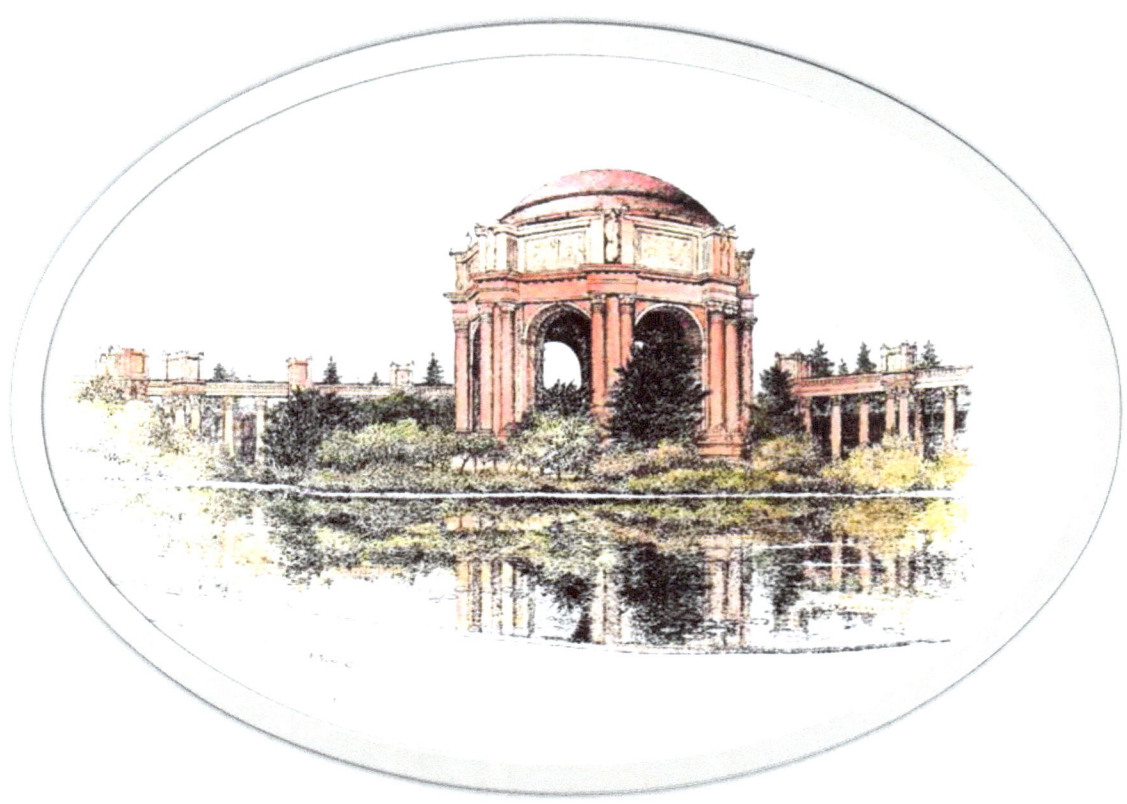

Palace of Fine Arts
San Francisco, California
Colored Pen & Ink

SAN FRANCISCO BAY AREA

"BEACHED AT BODEGA"

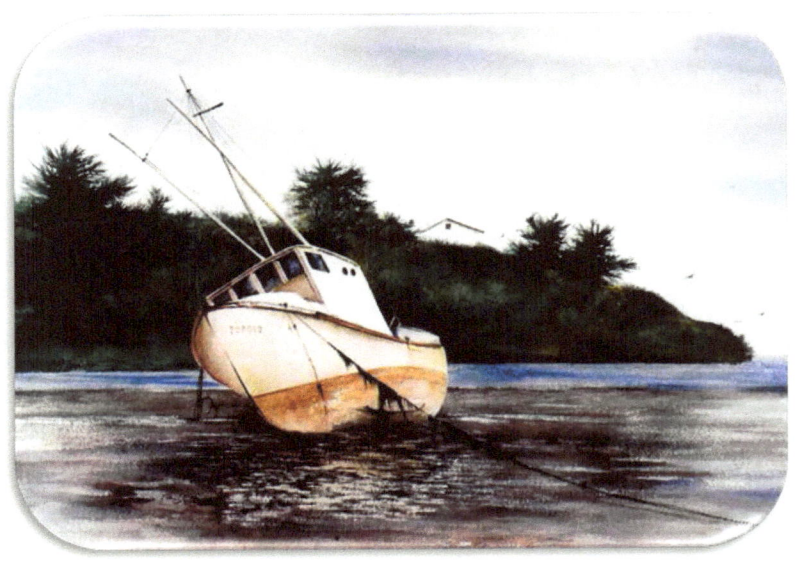

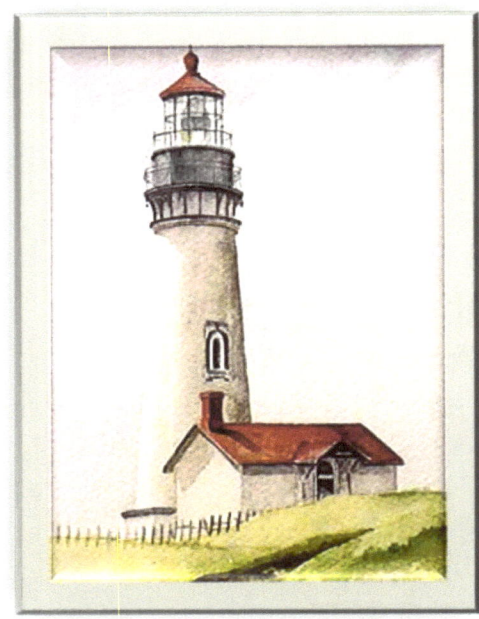

Bodega Bay, California
Famous for Alfred Hitchcock's movie,
"The Birds"

Pigeon Point Lighthouse
Pescadero, California

WEST COAST SCENES

MONTEREY, CALIFORNIA

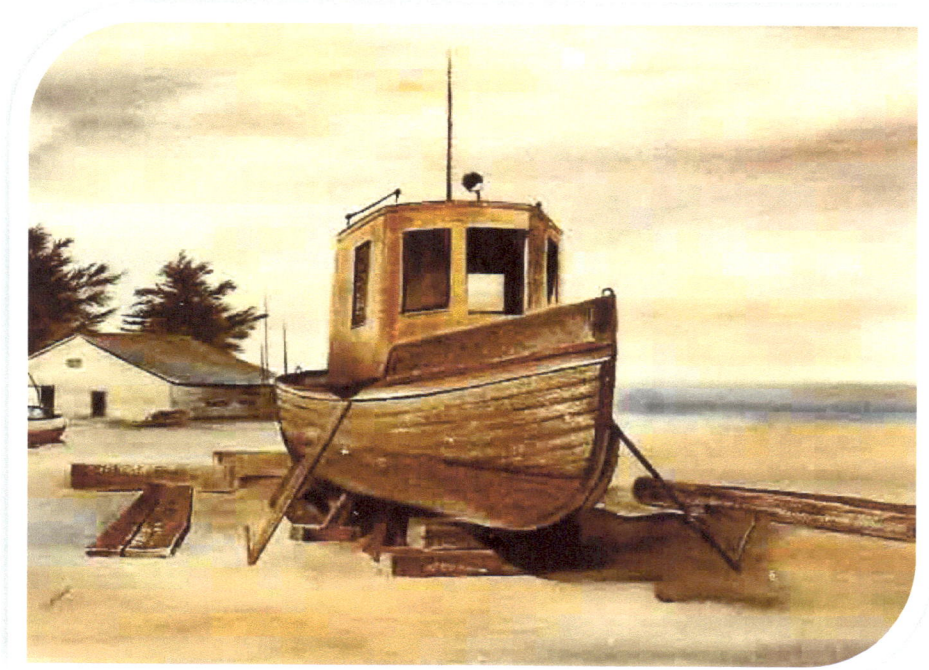

"MONTEREY BOATWORKS"

The watercolor painting shown above portrays an early scene at the Monterey Boat Works, a short distance from the famous Monterey Bay Aquarium on the way to Pacific Grove.

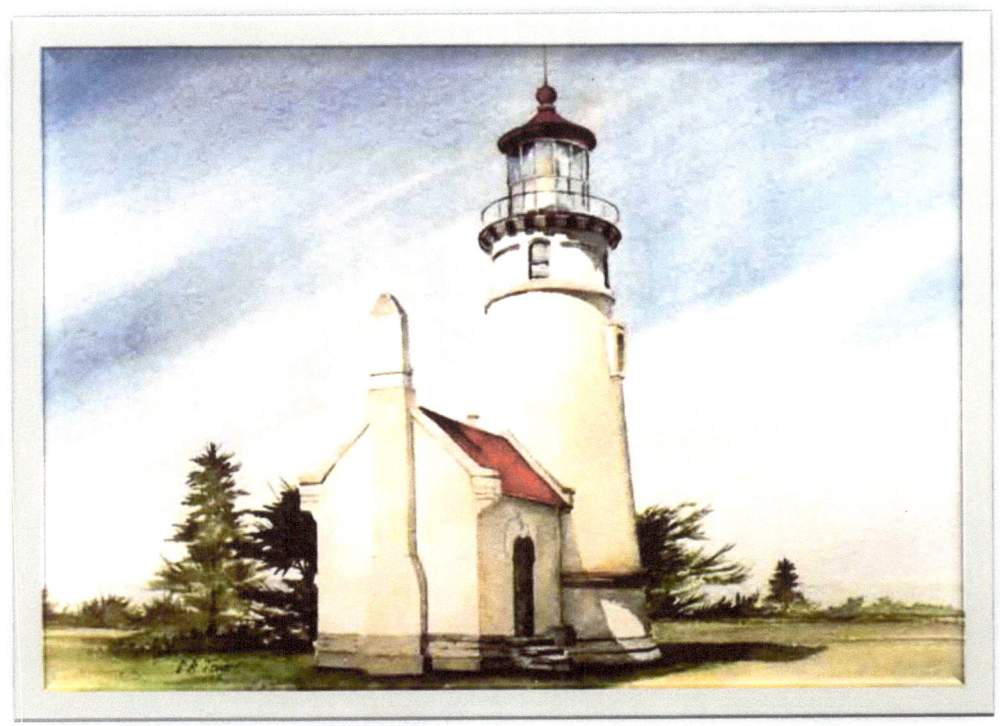

"UMPQUA RIVER LIGHTHOUSE" – Oregon Coast
A special stopping point on our trips north

WEST COAST SCENES

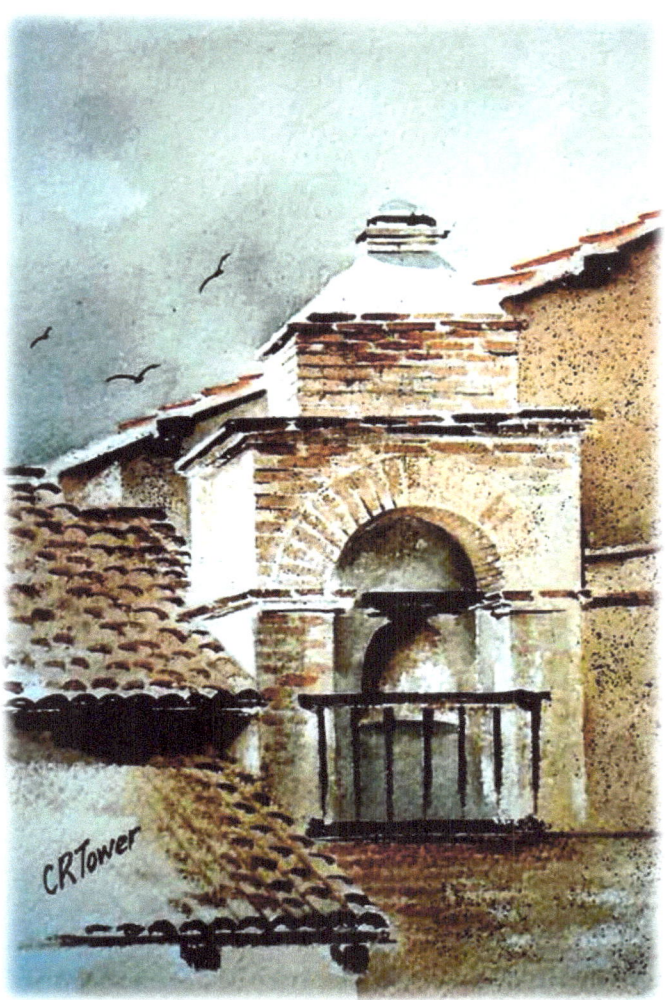 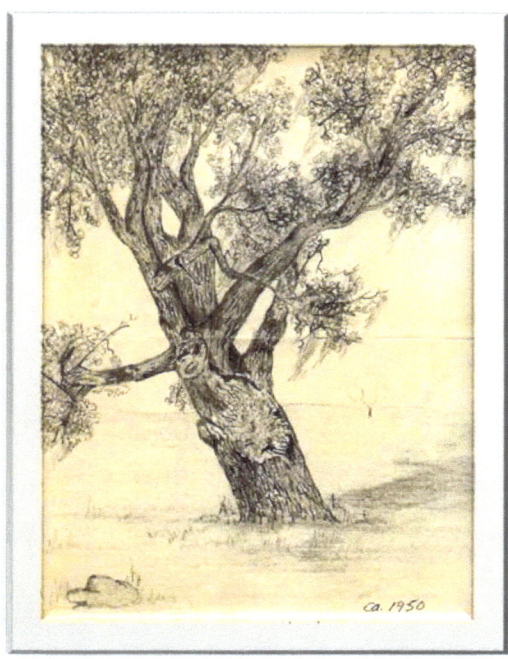

San Antonio de Padua (left) and following page, is located on California's Hunter Liggett Military Reservation where the California National Guard holds their annual summer training camp. While attending the camp in 1950, I found time to make the sketch above. As can be seen, my tendency toward fine detail was already working.

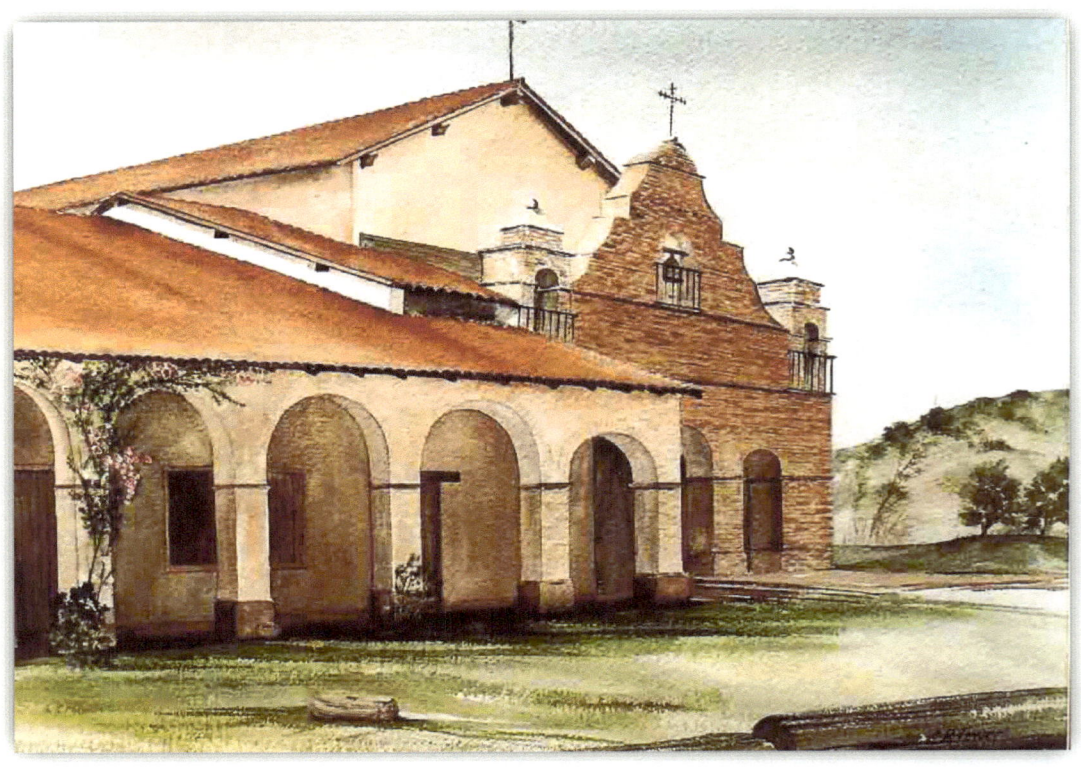

"MISSION SAN ANTONIO de PADUA"
One of California's 21 missions

MONUMENT VALLEY, UTAH

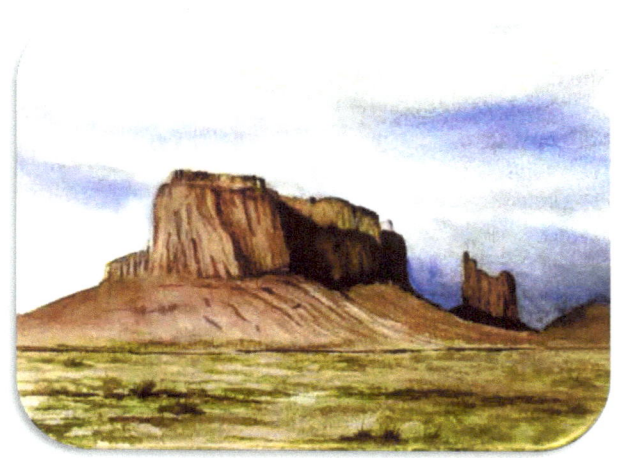

Following an intimidating drive through miles of barren loneliness, my late wife and I found ourselves entering the Valley immediately after a rare summer storm had washed across the landscape, leaving the Valley with the vivid colors seen in these paintings. It was a sight I will never forget and which I was compelled to paint.

"After the Storm – 1 & 2"

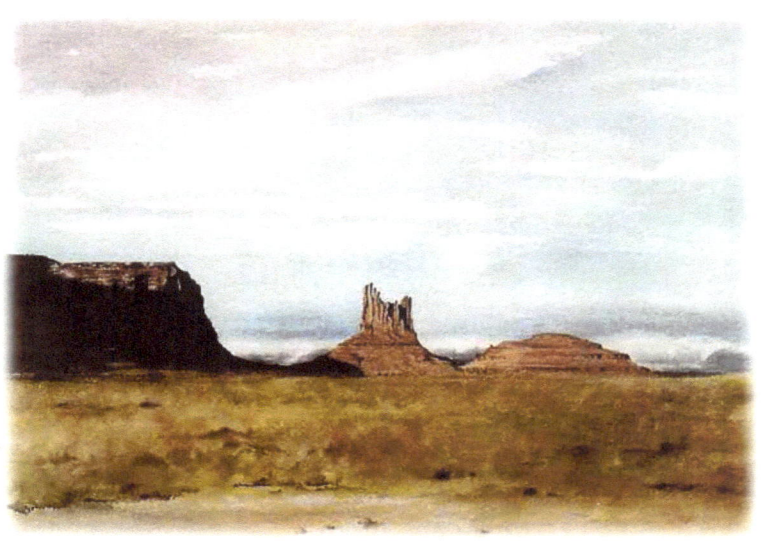

*Monument Valley,
A famous as a movie location for John Wayne movies,
was a "must-see" place on my bucket list.*

MONUMENT VALLEY, UTAH

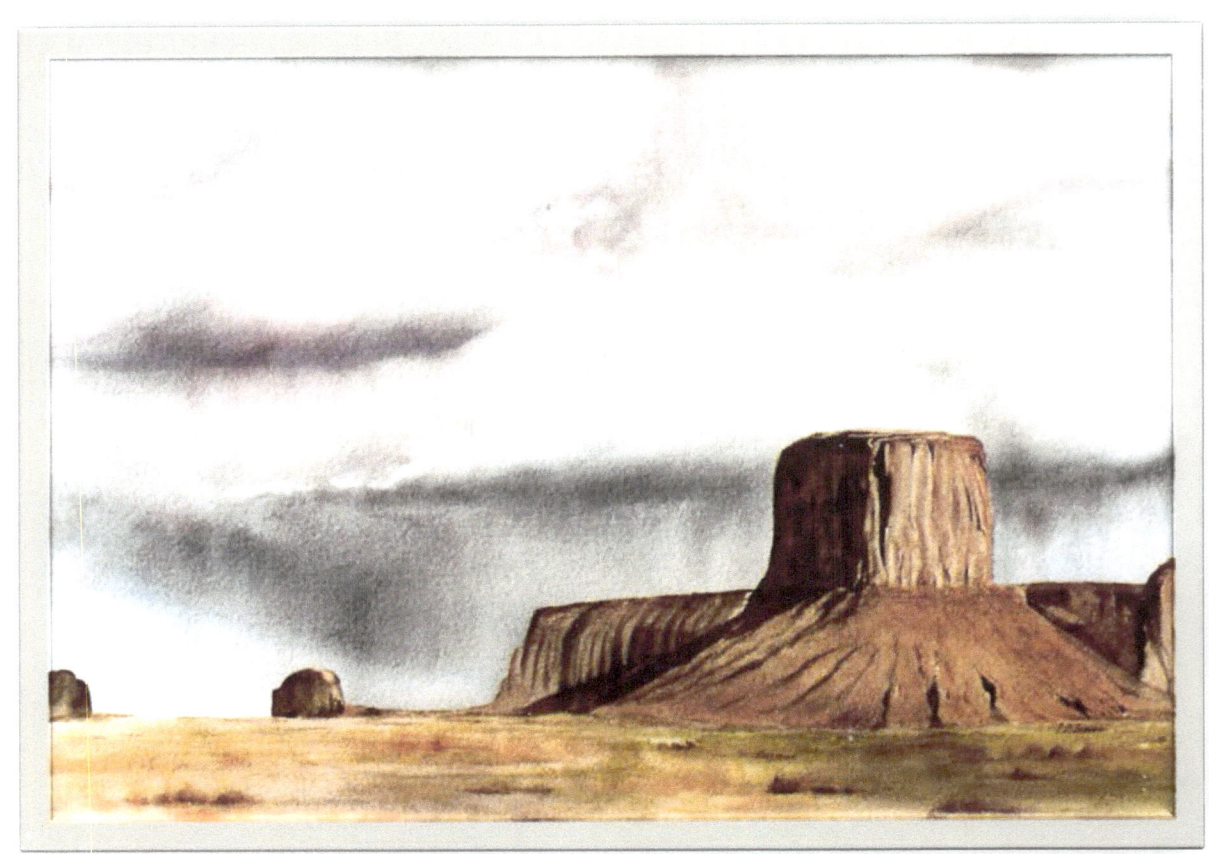

"After the Storm – 3"

TRAVELING ABROAD – FAVORITE PAINTINGS

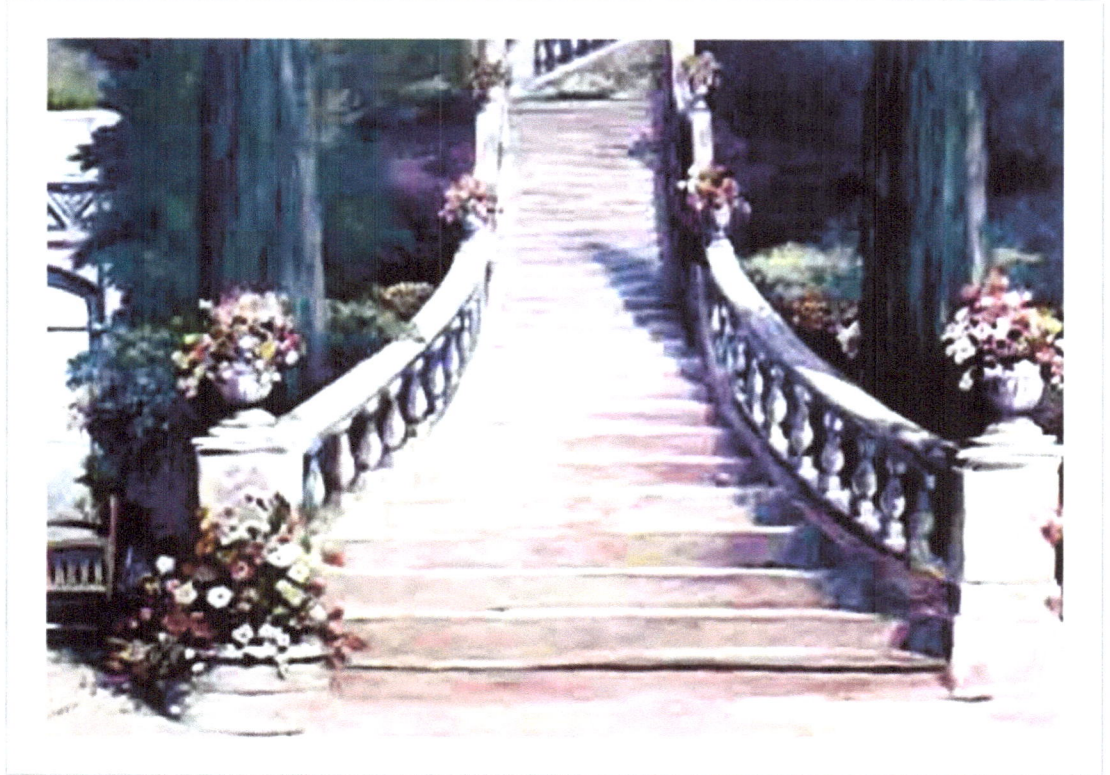

"STAIRWAY AT CASTLE COMBE"
England
Oil Painting

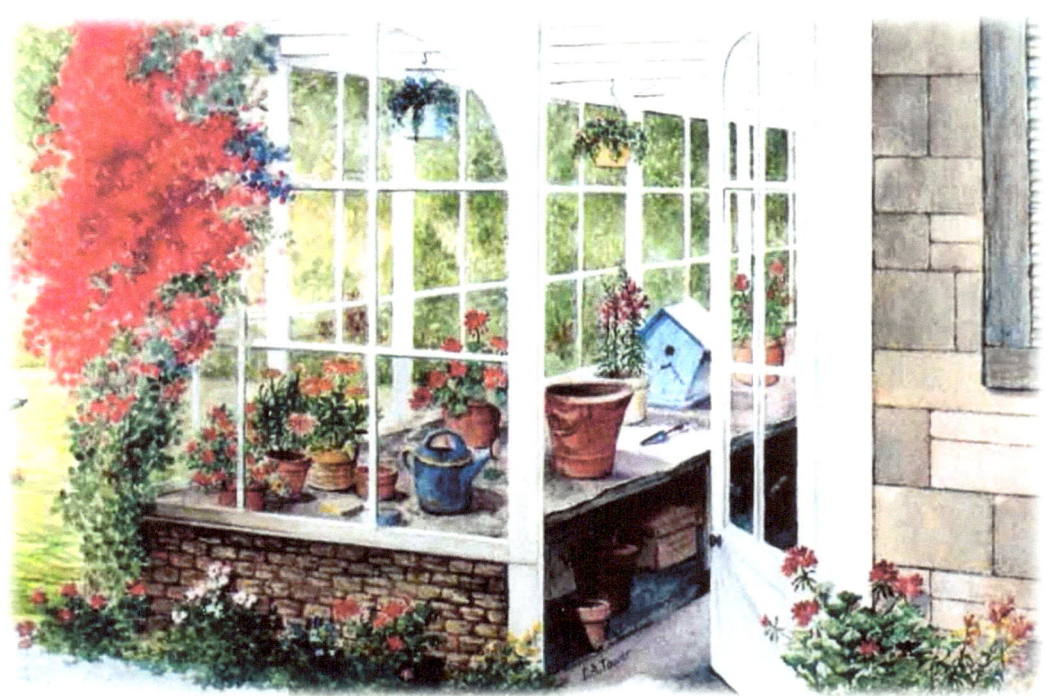

"GARDEN HOUSE AT CASTLE COMBE"
England
Watercolor

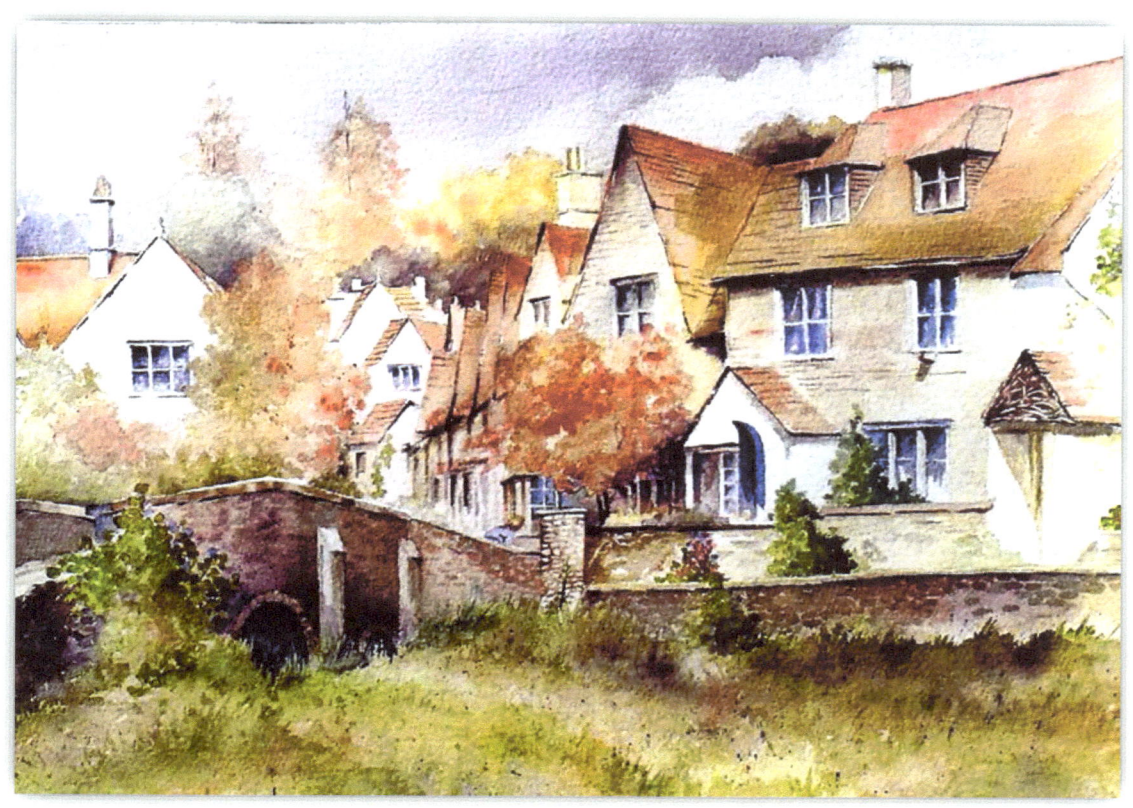

CASTLE COMBE - NORTH WILTSHIRE – ENGLAND
A primary scene location for 1967 movie "Doctor Doolittle"

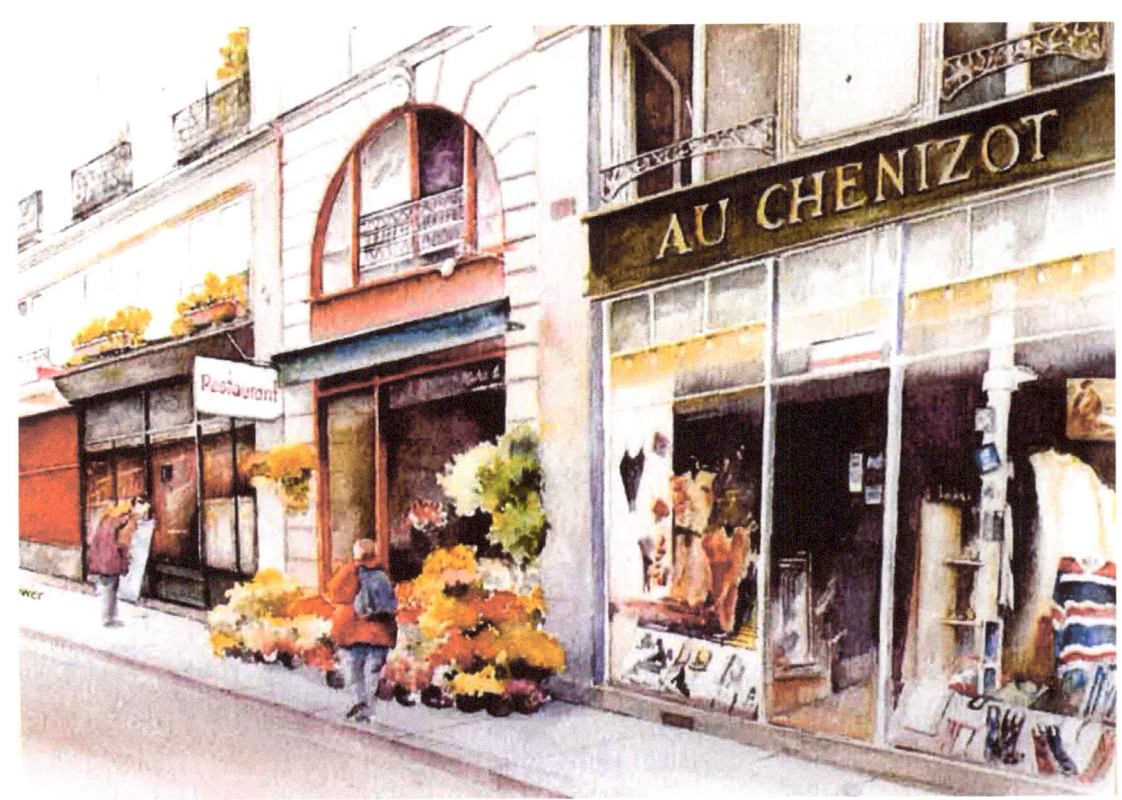

"AU CHENIZOT"
Paris, France
Watercolor

TRAVELING ABROAD – FAVORITE PAINTINGS AND DRAWINGS

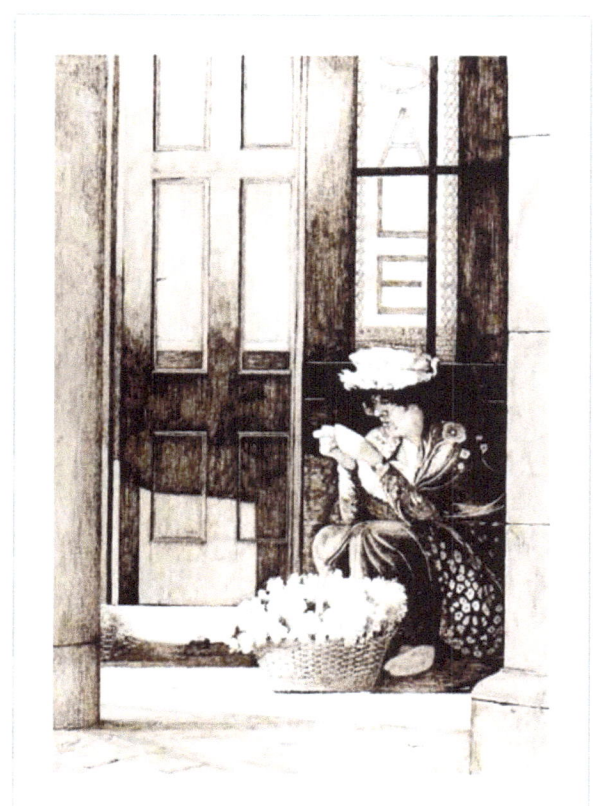

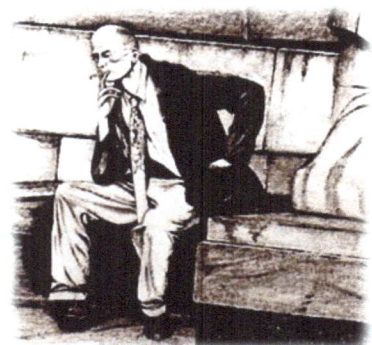

Detail of pen and ink drawing shown on following page.

The pen & ink drawings shown on this and the following page were completed on 3' x 4' canvas. Both were accomplished with a commercial "Sharpie" felt-tipped pen (fine black). Every stroke is the width of a "scratch." Lighter values were obtained by the use of pens that were 90% dry or more. If for any reason a mark was laid down that was too dark, such a mark could not be corrected.

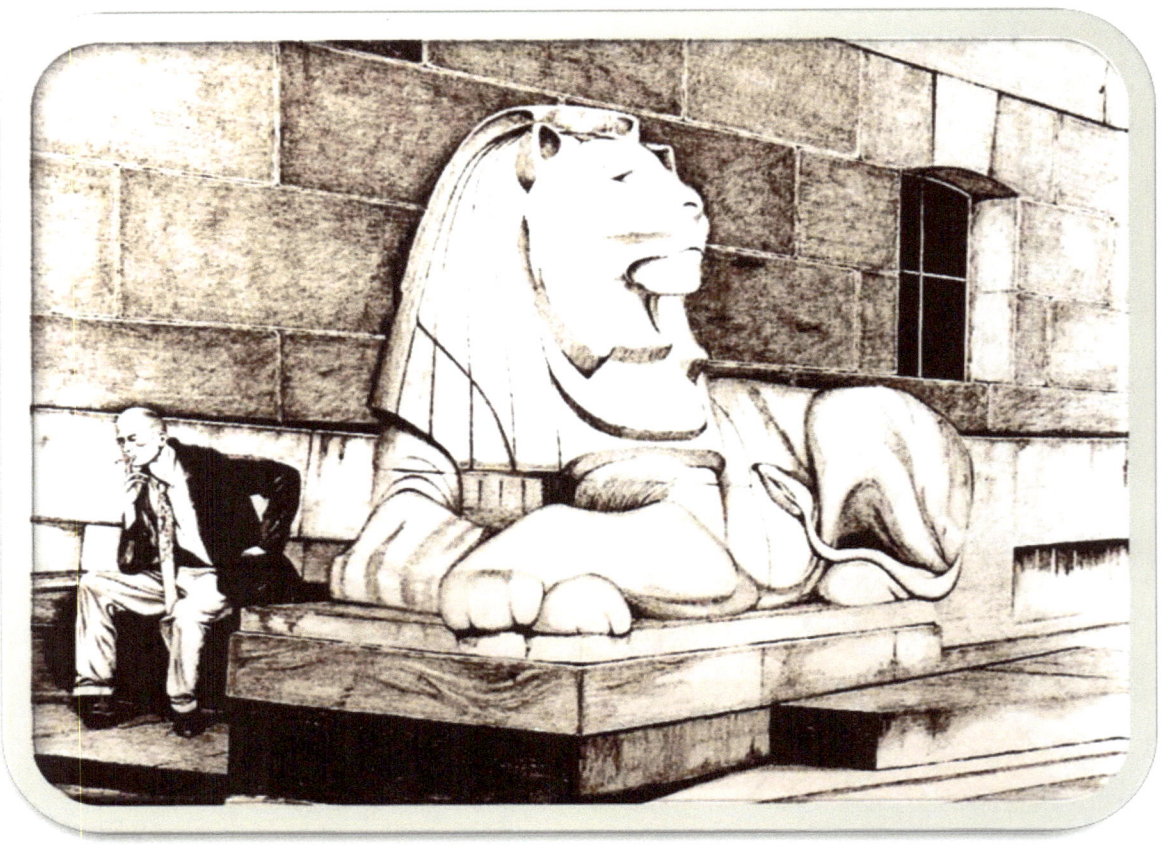

"SMOKING BREAK AT THE BRITISH MUSEUM"
Pen & Ink on canvas - 3' x 4'

WHAT PHOTOSHOP CAN DO FOR PUBLISHING

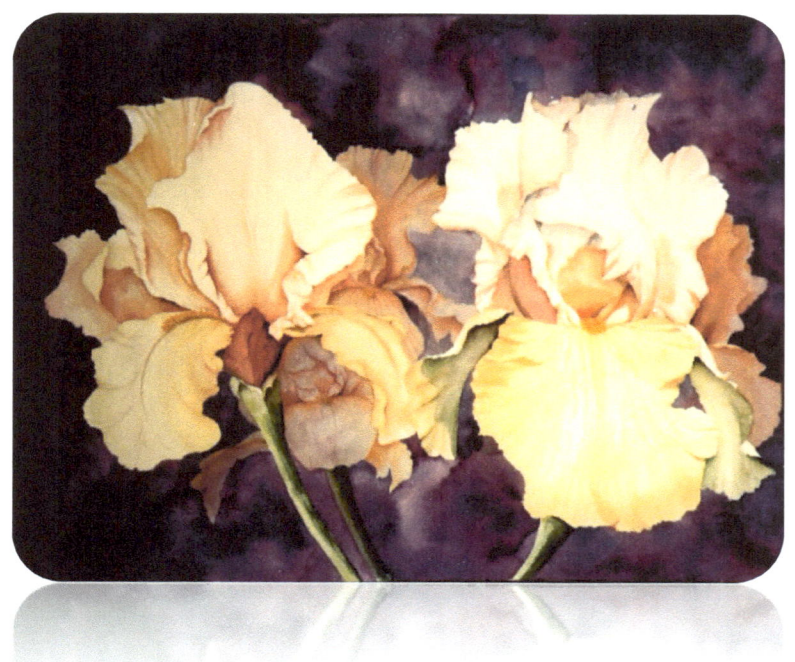

During World War II, as a young boy, I was employed by a local printing company that printed fruit and vegetable labels exclusively. I was fascinated by their overall beauty, so I pledged that I would someday design my own, just for the fun of it. This page and the following page show the results.

My efforts produced six fruit and flower designs overall, which were actually mass produced. I first designed and produced a background that allowed for the overprinting of the particular item, such as onions or flowers. Two examples are shown.

WHAT PHOTOSHOP CAN DO FOR PUBLISHING

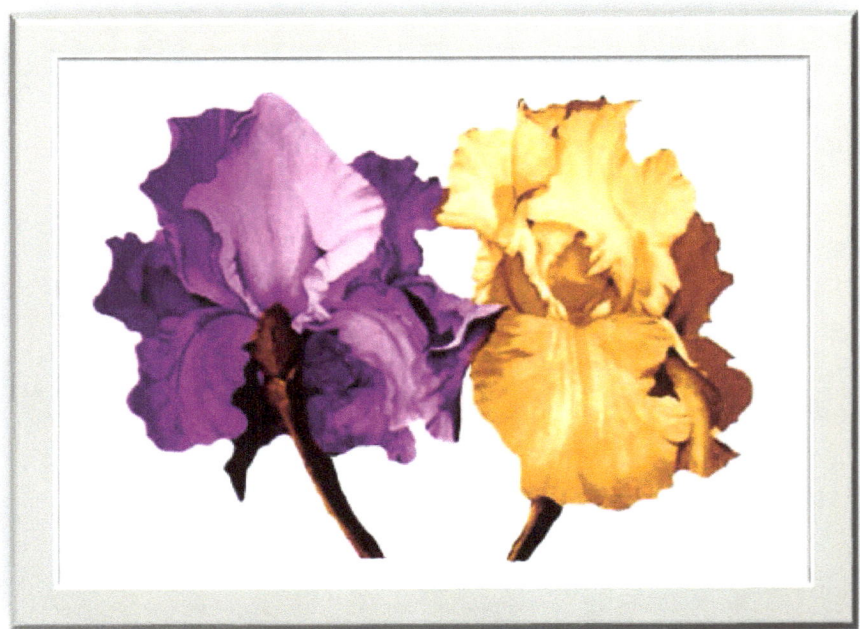

Using the iris design as an example, I started with the painting shown on the previous page and stripped away the entire digital background surrounding the flowers. This prepared me for the process of sliding the stripped image in place over my standardized background. Notice that I changed the color of the left flower. This entire process was made possible using Adobe Photoshop.

WHAT PHOTOSHOP CAN DO FOR PUBLISHING

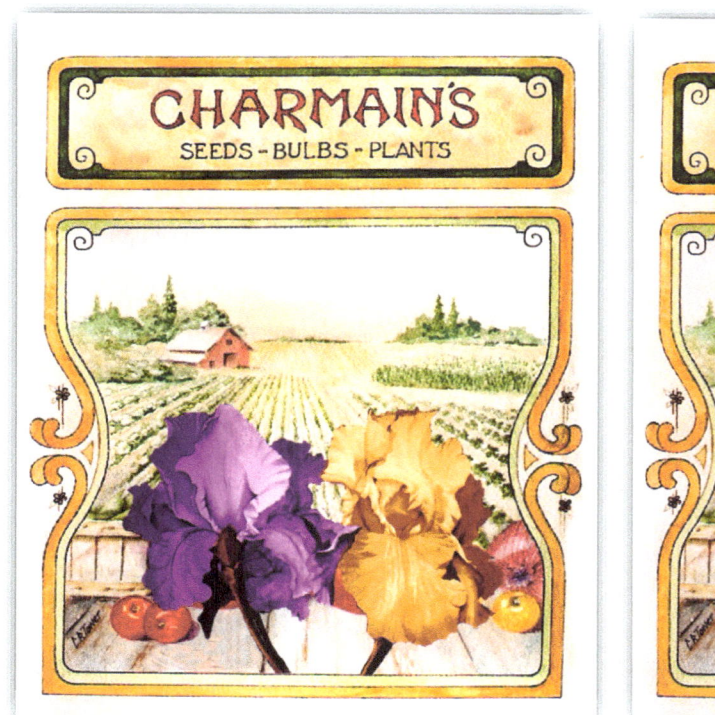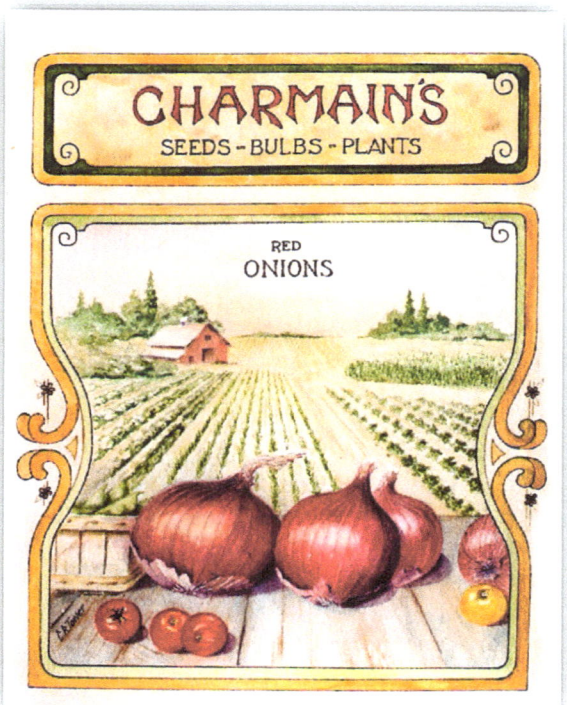

CHARMAIN'S SEEDS – IRIS and RED ONIONS"
(Notice identical backgrounds)

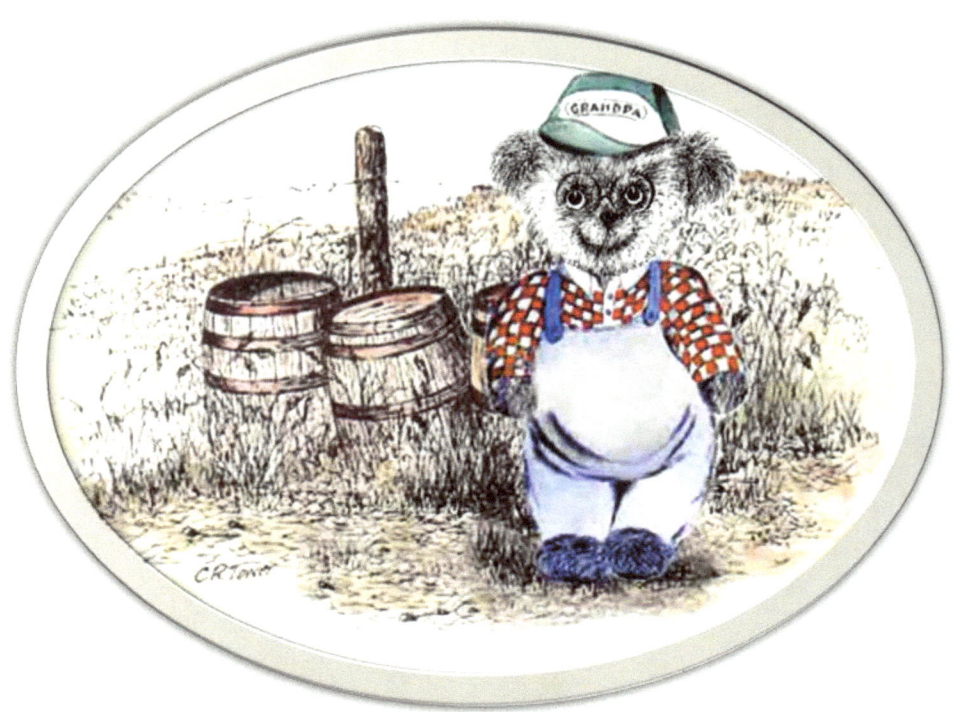

"GRANDPA BEAR AT THE BARRELS"
As with the seed packets, the Grandpa Bear image was merged
into a separate existing background by using Adobe Photoshop.

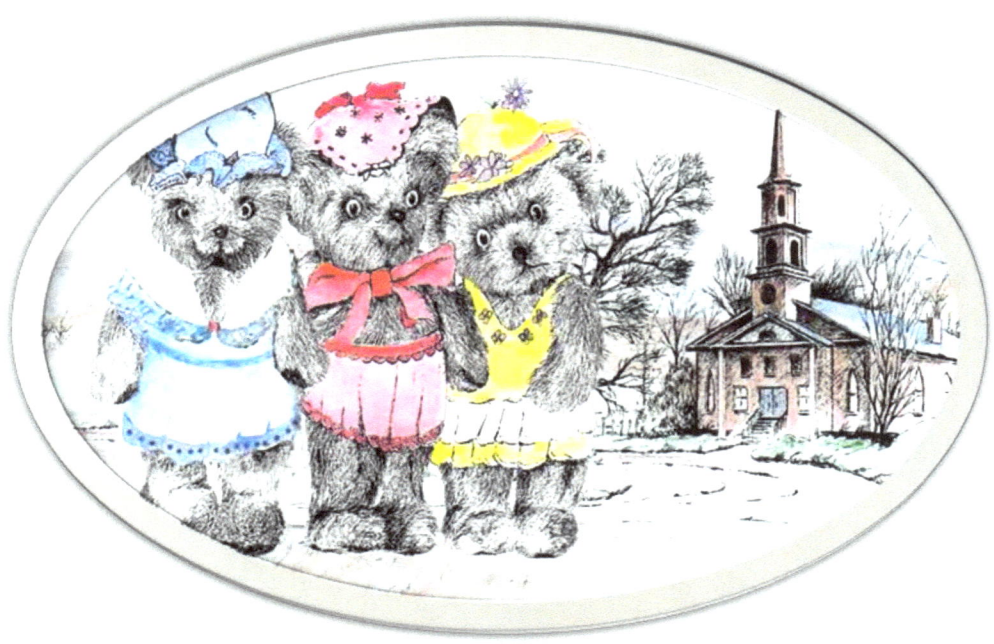

"THE THREE BEARS AT CHURCH"
As with the seed packets, the Three-Bear image was merged into a separate existing background by using Adobe Photoshop.

MORE PHOTOSHOP EXTRAS – OVERLAPPING IMAGES

The full-color carousel horse with rider shown on the following page, (Image 5) is a Photoshop composite from my children's book. (Image 1, shown below, was available for use, but I needed one with much more pizzazz. To save the work of preparing a completely new image, I decided to create this Photoshopped composite from bits and pieces.

(Image 2), shown below, was also in my files and available for use, but was clearly not what I wanted. The following describes how I combined elements to arrive at the final image 5:

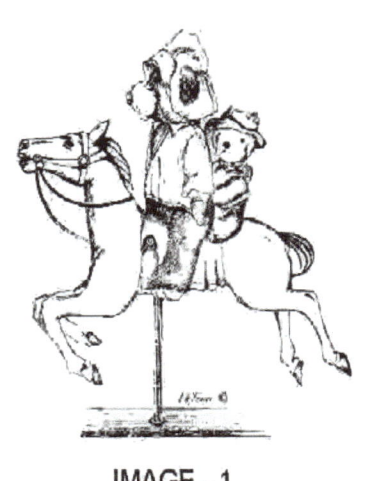

IMAGE - 1

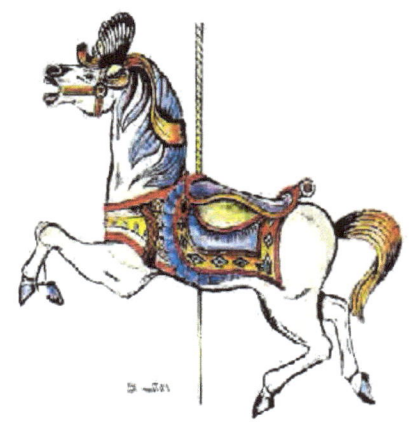

IMAGE - 2

The first step required stripping away the entire digital background surrounding the targeted image. (See Image 3). All of this was made possible by Adobe Photoshop software. The next step required sliding the stripped image to its new location. (See Image 4 for this result). (Image 3 is shown uncolored for clarification purposes). Once accomplished, the resulting image 3 was then colored and moved into position by means of the amazing Adobe Photoshop.

MORE PHOTOSHOP EXTRAS – OVERLAPPING IMAGES

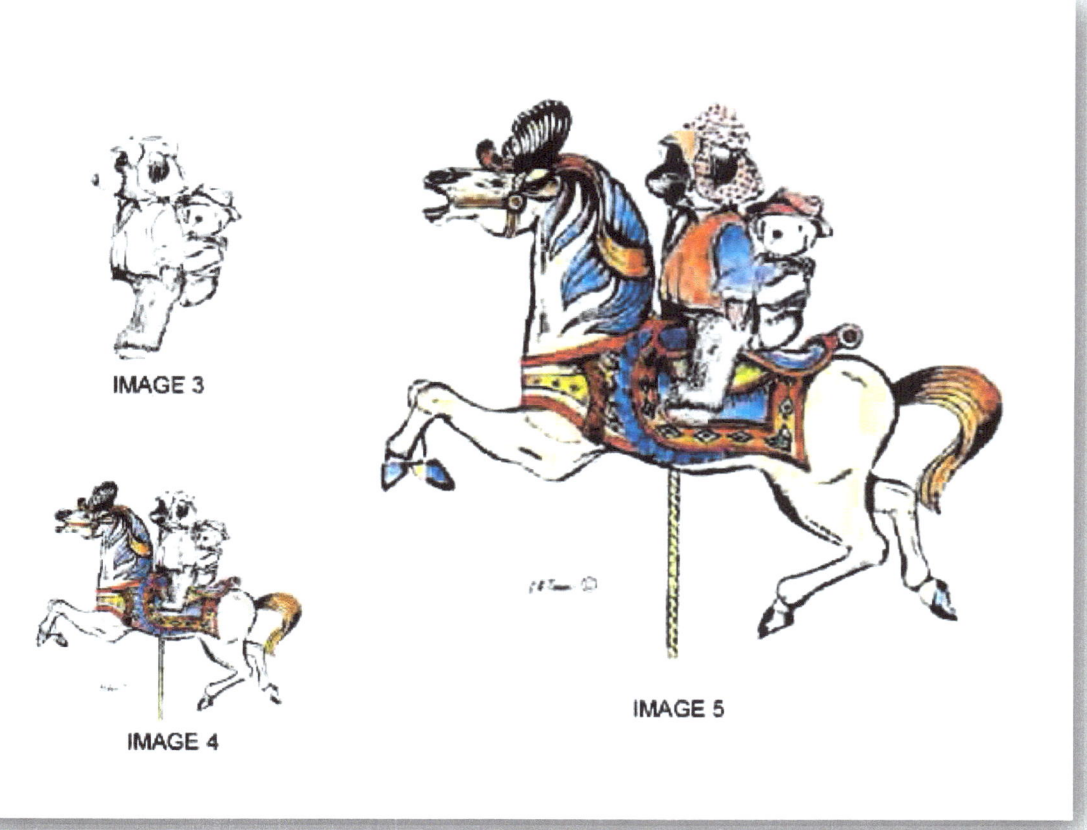

IMAGE 3

IMAGE 4

IMAGE 5

IMAGES FROM MY OUTDOOR DAYS
Sierra Nevada fishing streams, along with the California Delta waterways, provided most of my outdoor memories.

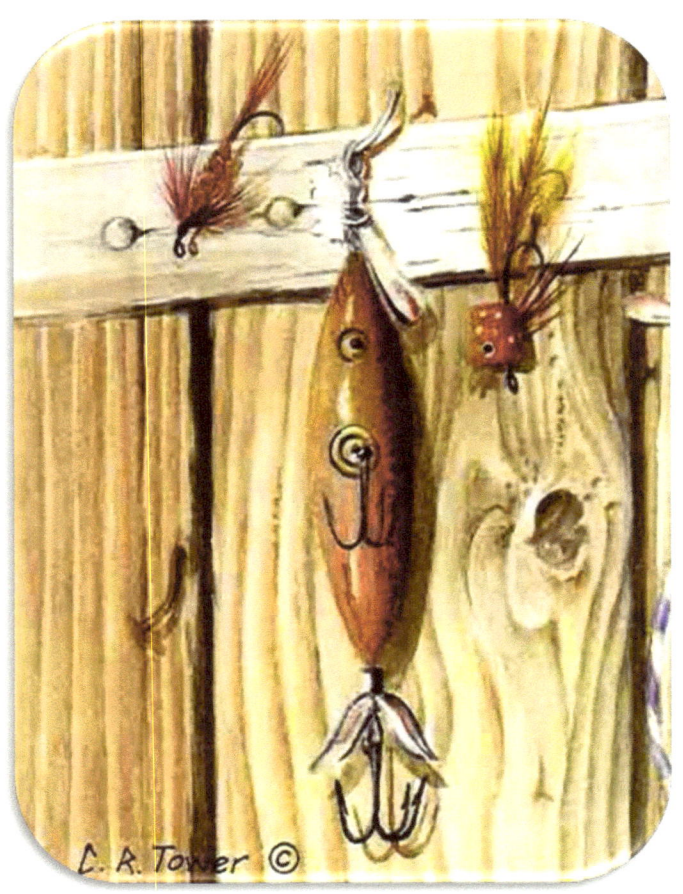

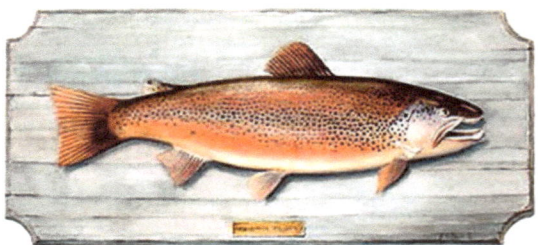

Personal gear was used in many of these paintings.

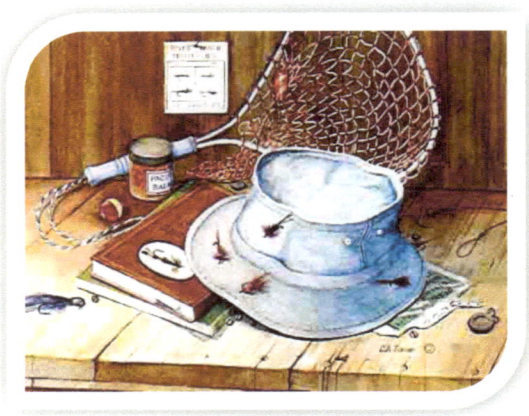

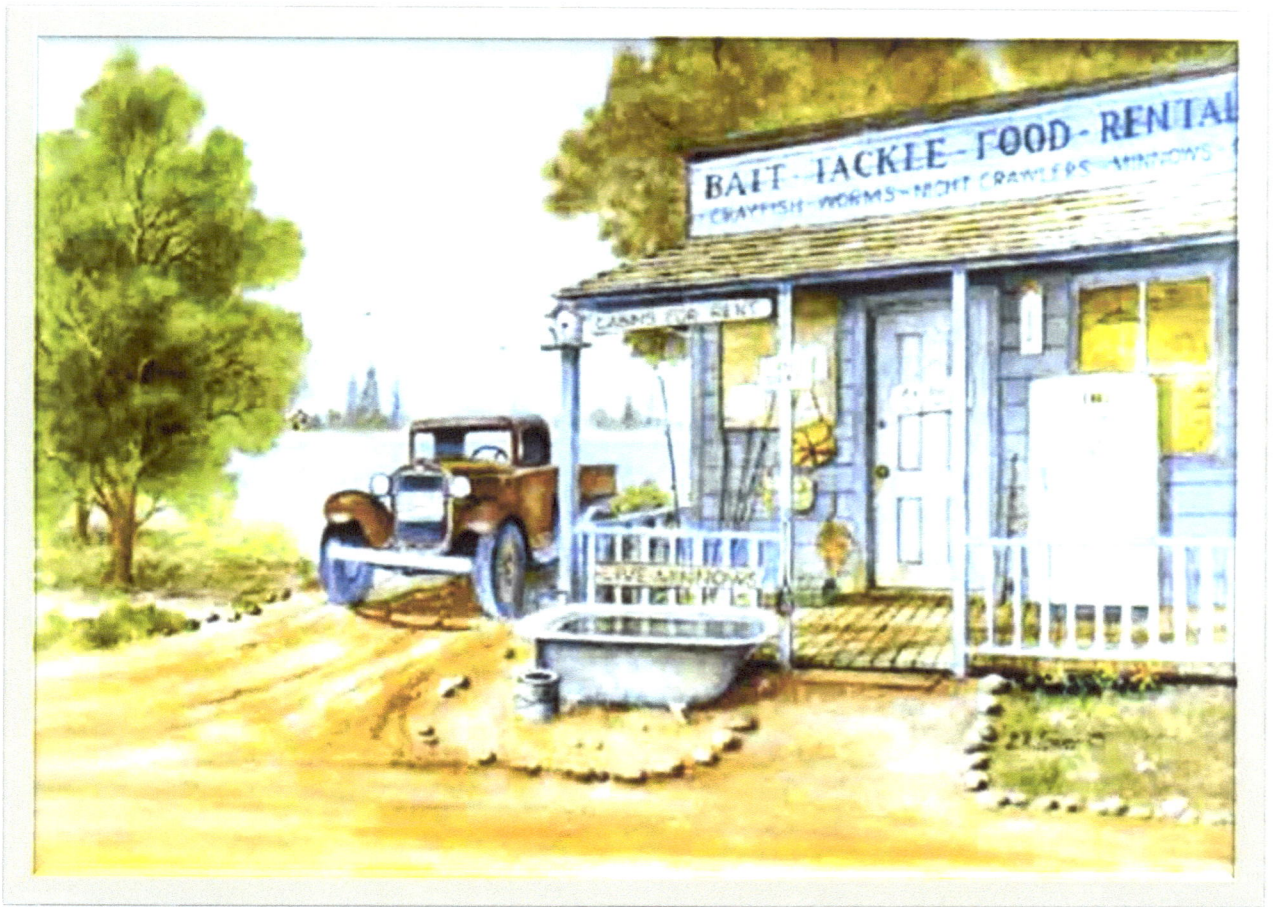

"THE BLUE BAIT HOUSE"
Water Color
(Always wanted a Bait Shop)

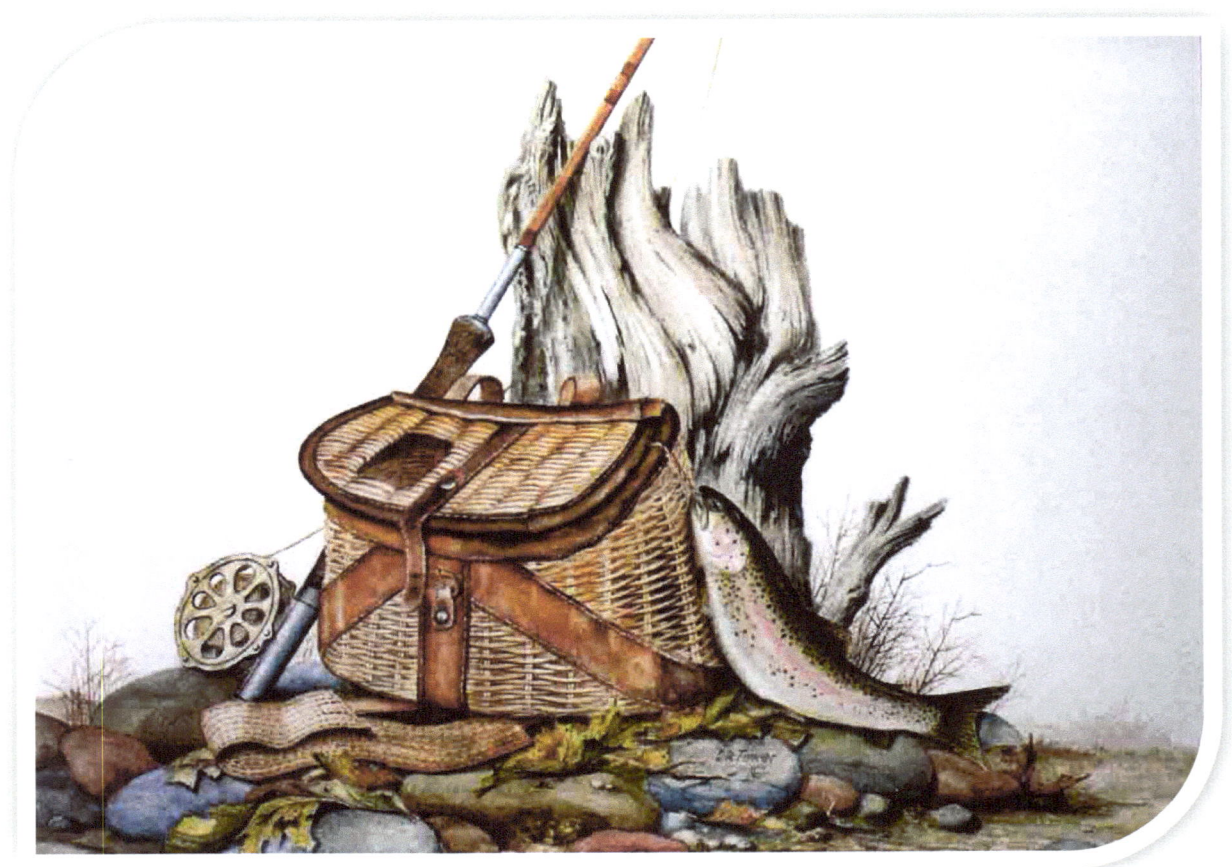

"After the Catch – 1"
(Again, from my own gear)

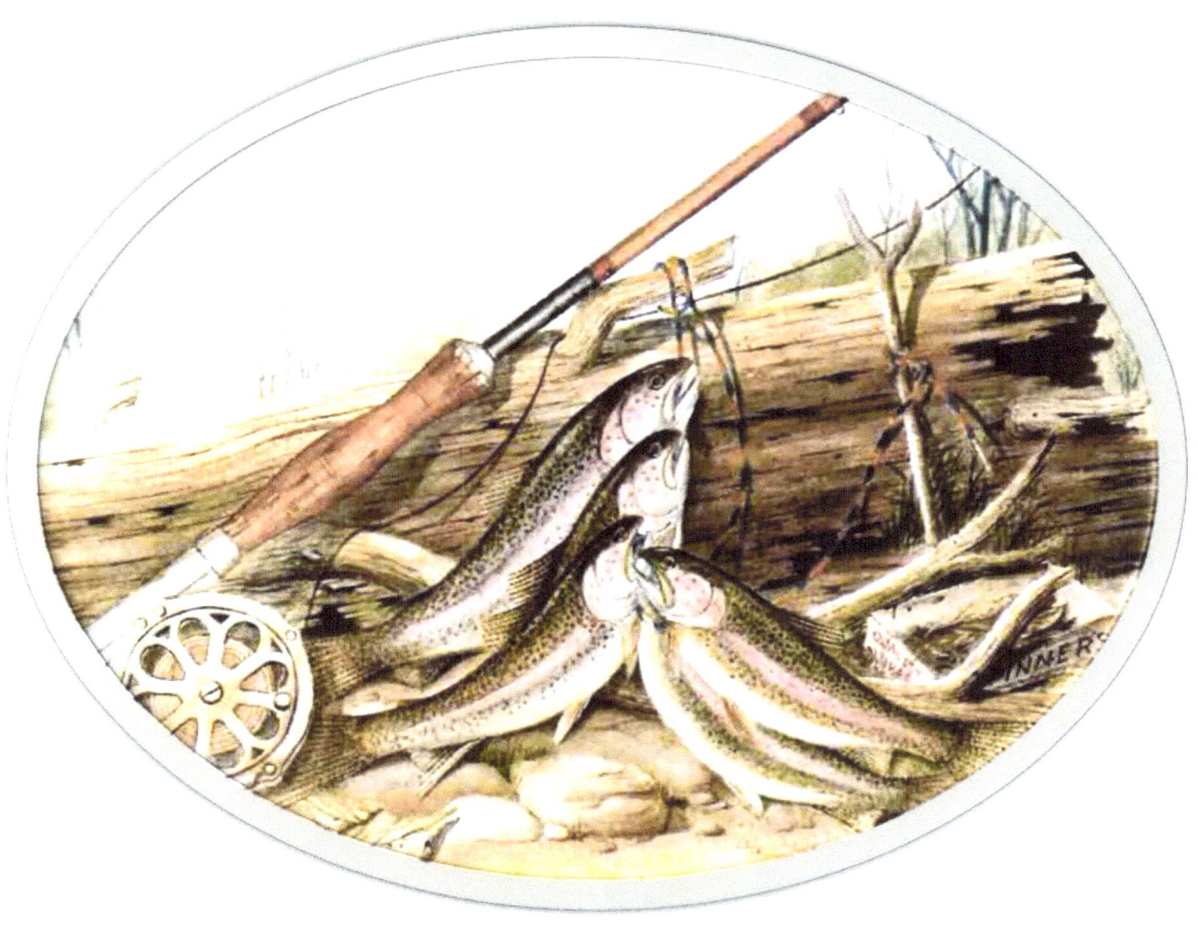

"After the Catch – 2"
(Again, from my own gear)

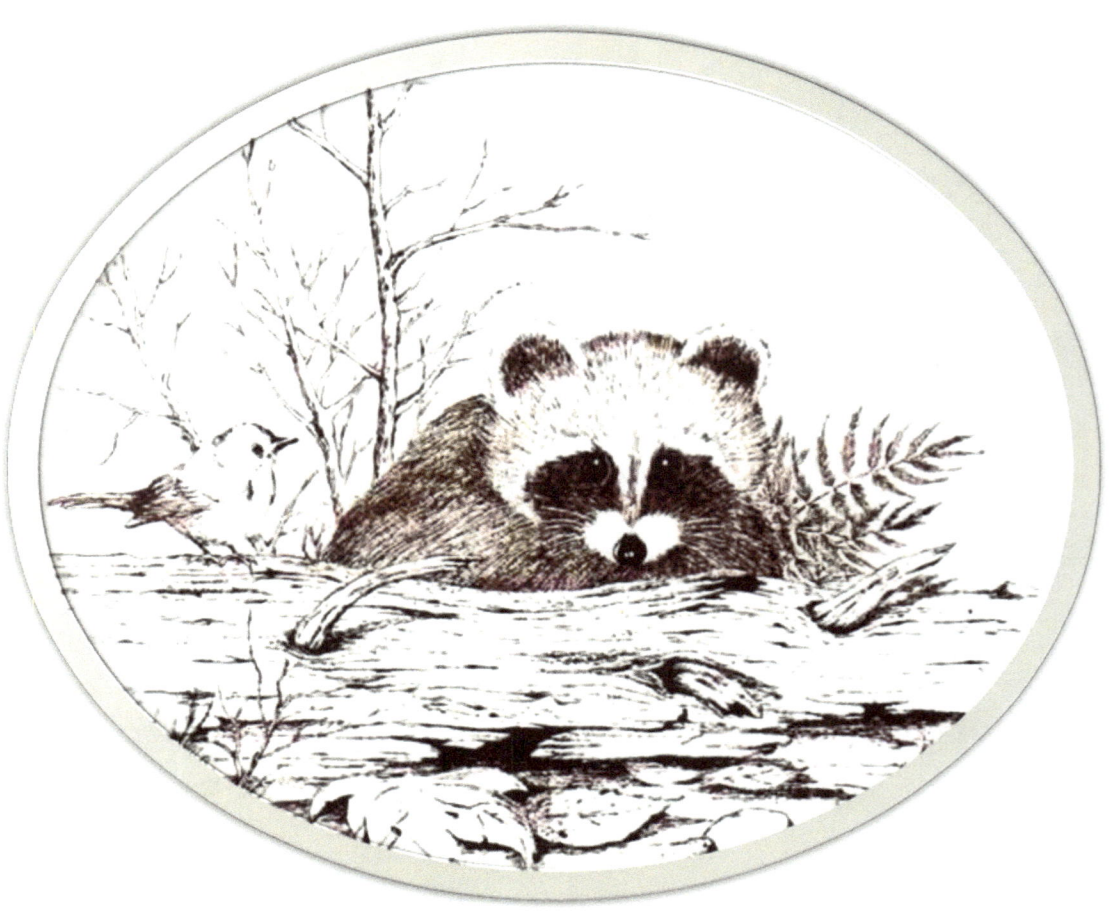

"A Backyard Friend"
Once seen often – not seen at all any more.

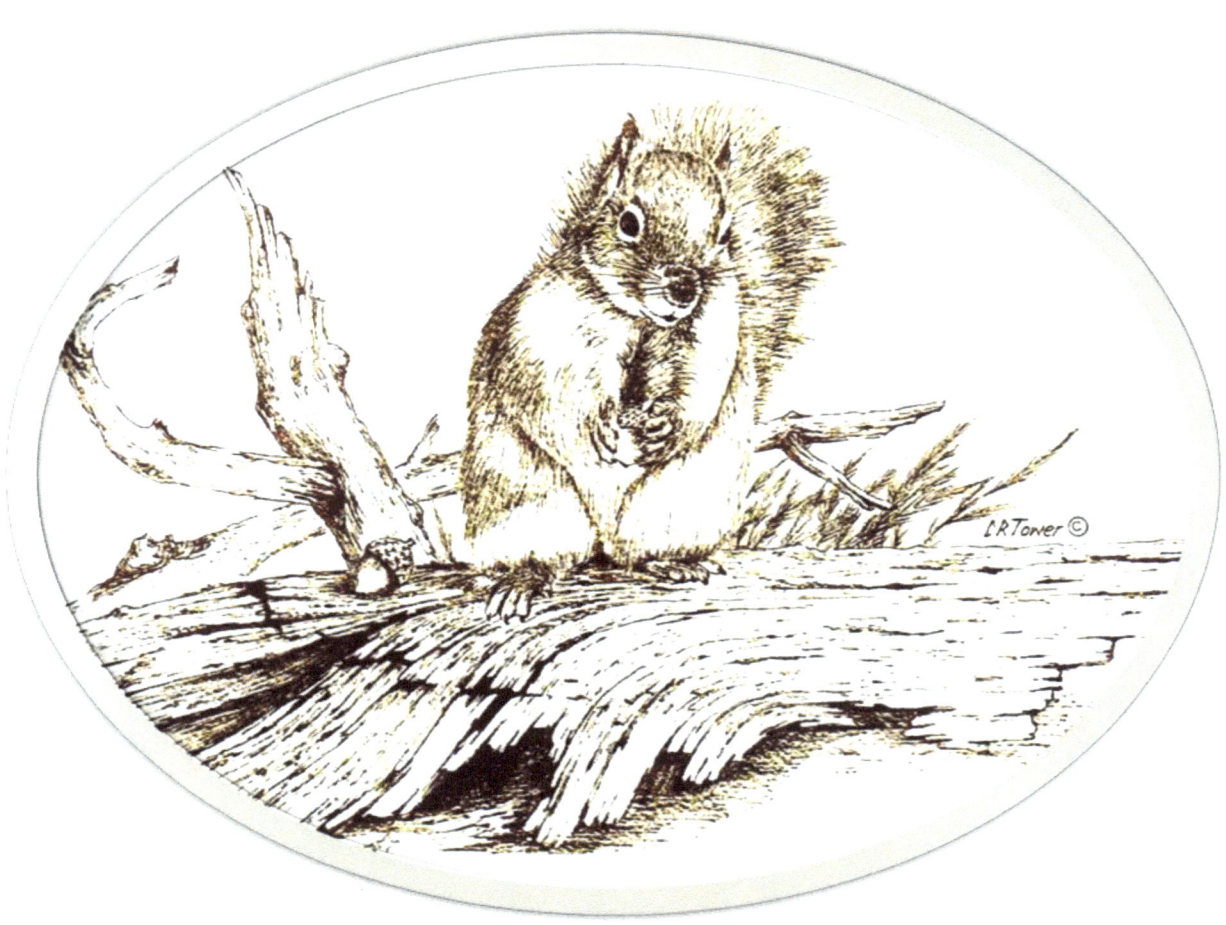

"A Backyard Friend – 2"

(This guy's decedents are still around!)

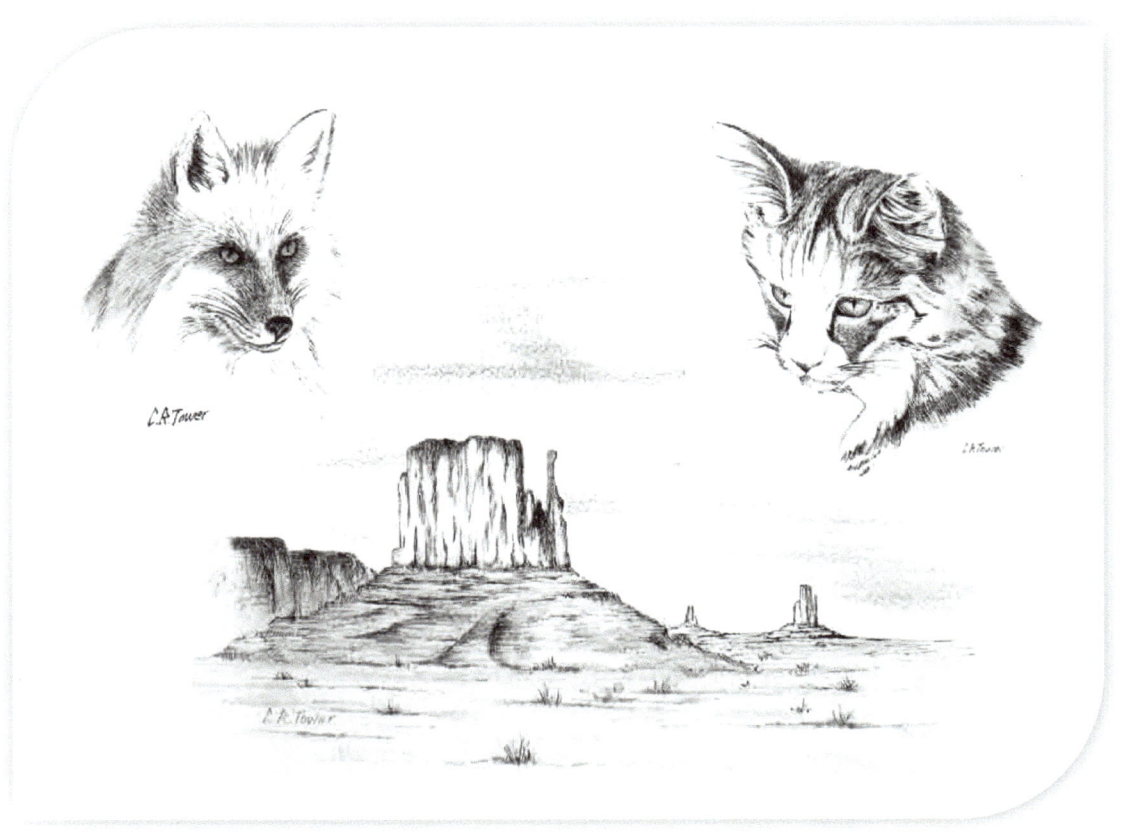

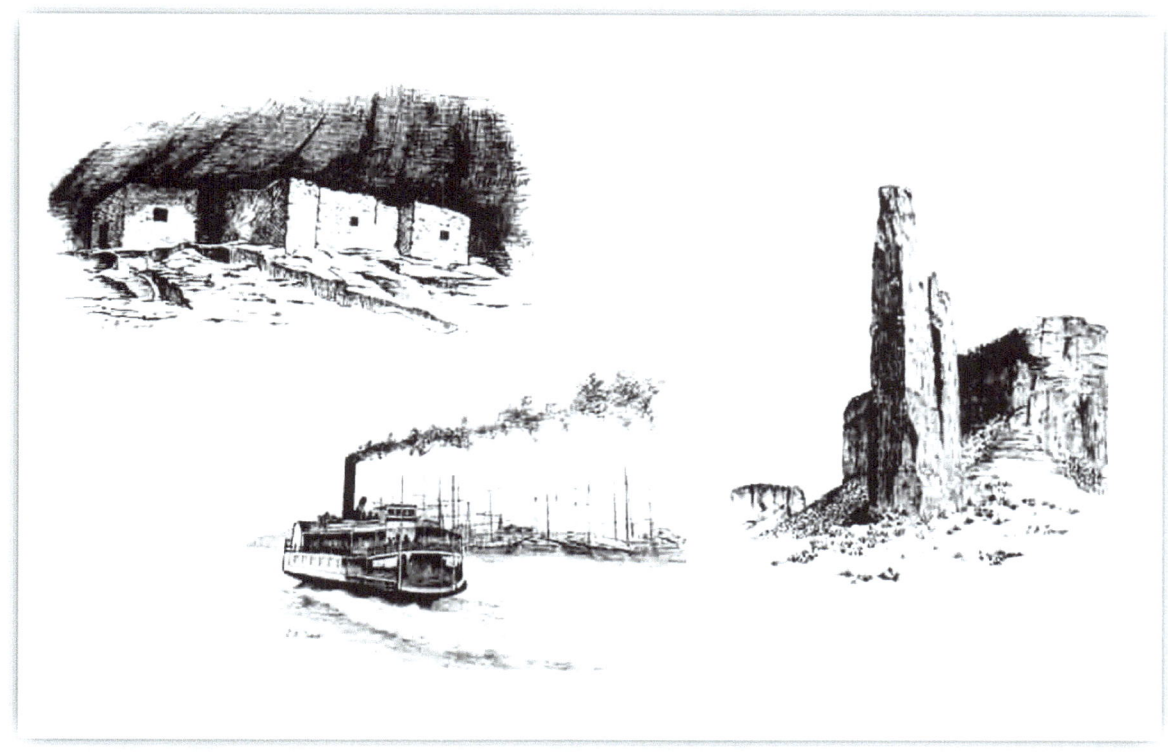

PEN & INK - PAINTED ON LOCATION – COLORED LATER

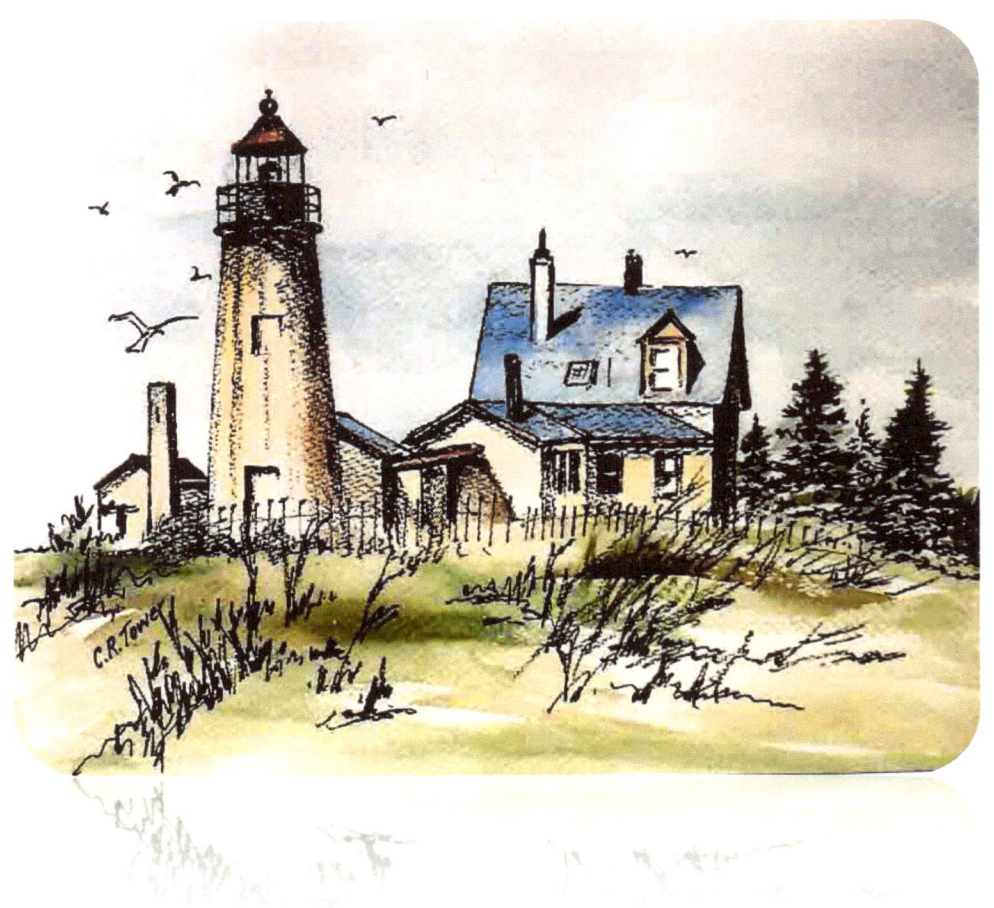

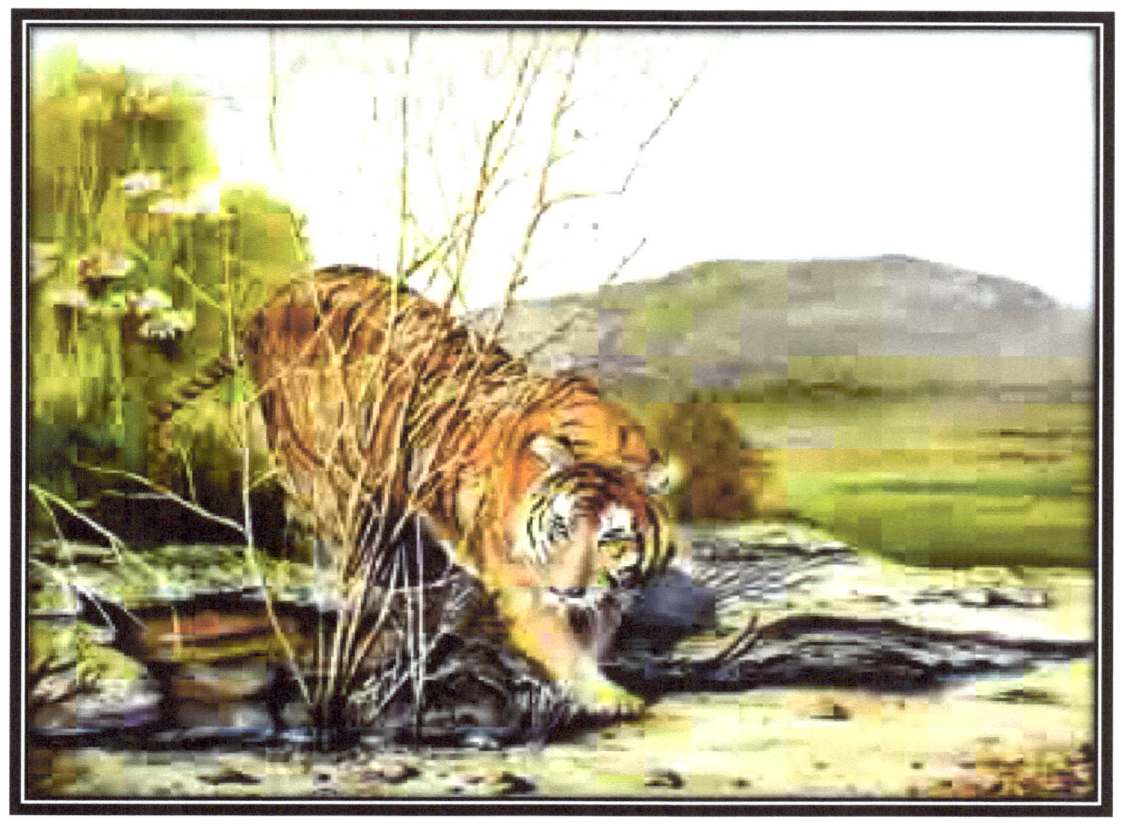

A trip to the zoo was the motivation for this watercolor.
One of my favorites!

THE END

ABOUT THE ARTIST

Clarence Robert Tower is a lifelong resident of California's Silicon Valley. He is a self-taught artist, but can claim brief contributions to the commercial art profession with book illustrations and artistic contributions to Muscular Dystrophy national campaigns. (See drawing below). Mr. Tower spent his professional years as a Civil engineer and Licensed Land Surveyor during the Silicon Valley's growing years. As unusual as it might seem, this profession afforded major contributions to his art career. Prior to the emergence of computer technology, engineering plans and official subdivision maps were accomplished entirely by hand with old-style pens that were hand-loaded with India Ink and subsequently applied to starched linen. With that being the case, preparing these maps made up a major portion of an engineer's responsibilities. Engineering firms in those early years were somewhat judged by the artistry of their recorded documents. To keep up with competition, engineers were compelled to become better than average artists.

After completing his published books, Seventy Years in the Silicon Valley, an Anecdotal History, The Adventures of Zack Gentry, a Tongue and Cheek History of the Opening of the West, a children's book, The Life of a Teddy Bear Family, and an Arcadia Publications book, Legendary Locals of Santa Clara, he realized he had accumulated an immense stock of digital images and image-building information he could pass on. This book satisfies this capability.

This drawing was used nationwide by Muscular Dystrophy.

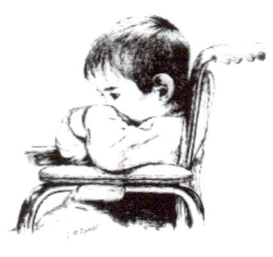